Ghosts Among Us

Ghosts Among Us

*Uncovering the Truth
About the Other Side*

James Van Praagh

HarperOne
An Imprint of HarperCollinsPublishers

HarperOne

HarperCollins books may be purchased for educational, business, or sales promotional use. For information please write: Special Markets Department, HarperCollins Publishers, 10 East 53rd Street, New York, NY 10022.

HarperCollins Web site: http://www.harpercollins.com
HarperCollins®, 🐿®, and HarperOne™ are
trademarks of HarperCollins Publishers

FIRST HARPERCOLLINS PAPERBACK EDITION PUBLISHED IN 2009

Designed by Level C

Library of Congress Cataloging-in-Publication Data

Van Praagh, James.
Ghosts among us : uncovering the truth about the other side /
James Van Praagh.
p. cm.
ISBN 978-0-06-155338-7
1. Spiritualism. 2. Van Praagh, James. 3. Ghosts. I. Title.
BF1301.V36   2008
133.9′1—dc22   2008003077

09 10 11 12 13 RRD (H) 10 9 8 7 6 5 4 3 2 1

To Patricia Ford Bodine
My very first mentor, who taught me that a good ghost story is
not just one that you read, but one that you live.

Contents

Introduction

You are reading this book right now because you have a curiosity about ghosts, spirit communication, or the afterlife. Never before has there been such an overwhelming curiosity in all things ghostly. More and more people share a deep desire for such knowledge and a sincere interest in developing their expertise in the field. I believe that as a society we have evolved spiritually to abandon preconceived notions and step away from the back parlor séance rooms and gauze matted forms and open our minds to the truth about the misunderstood and elusive world of ghosts.

Today ghosts are in the same position that mediumship and spirit communication held over ten years ago. When my first book, *Talking to Heaven*, became number one on the *New York Times* best-seller list in 1997, it was touted as the "book that took the publishing world by storm." From its initial modest printing of 6,000 copies, it quickly climbed to 600,000 copies in the following two months. I believe that the book's success was a direct result of my appearance on *Larry King Live* on December 13, 1997. It was the first time a medium had ever appeared as a guest on

Larry's show, and the first time spiritual messages from the dead were relayed to an international audience. I was told that the phone lines were jammed while I was on the show and that people continued to call for days after the broadcast aired. After such a response, the producers of the show asked me back, and two weeks later I appeared on *Larry King Live* again. I was subsequently asked to appear on every major daytime TV and radio show.

Obviously, I had struck a chord. Everywhere I went, people wanted to know if their deceased relatives were around them, if I knew what they were doing, and if I could see dead people all the time. It seemed that the public could not get their fill of talking to the dead. In turn, many people shared with me their own experiences of spirit communication. It was as if the book gave people the right to embrace an issue that had been considered taboo, and almost overnight the subject of speaking to the dead became the latest fad. Mediums began popping up like crazy. More books were written, more television shows were produced, and more movies were filmed depicting the world of mediums.

This same trend is occurring today with ghosts.

Ghosts are now part of the mainstream. One can no longer ignore the fact that people have an ongoing phantasm love affair with ghosts. A multitude of shows all over the globe are taking up real estate on the television airwaves. One can go ghost-busting, experience a haunting, and witness a spirit possession all in a single afternoon. While the world enjoys this newly popular ghostly entertainment, ghosts can be mischievous and cause major havoc to an unsuspecting aspirant who ignorantly ventures into their unseen world.

When I was developing my show *The Ghost Whisperer* in 2004, I felt a strong sense of responsibility to portray the world of ghosts as accurately as possible, because television is not only a means to entertain but also a tool to educate. After receiving six hundred e-mails asking whether everything in *The Ghost Whisperer* was true, I felt a sense of obligation to set the record straight about the complexities and simplicities of the ghostly side of life. In writing this book, my hope was to give you, the reader, a new understanding and appreciation of the unseen forces that, although dead, are still very much a part of your daily life. I want you to be able to distinguish truth from fiction, insights from embellishments.

During the past twenty-five years, I have listened to and witnessed the wanderings of thousands upon thousands of ghosts existing in places one couldn't even imagine. Those experiences have made me keenly aware of the intricacies of the human experience and the lingering results of mental and emotional anguish.

Science is all well and good, but when you can get firsthand information from a ghost, it doesn't get much better than that. This subject takes on a whole new level of understanding when the understanding and words come directly from the ghosts who are haunting us. Many people ask where the ghost world is. Are they always around us? Do they see everything? My desire is to provide insight and examples of how we share our space with ghosts and to show that they are a part of everyone's life. By becoming more aware of ghosts and spirits, we learn that sensing the other dimensions around us is not an experience limited to an exclusive group of people but one available to us all. Simply put, there is more power in knowledge and awareness than ignorance.

When I was a little boy, I knew I was different. I had been seeing ghosts from the time I was lying in a crib. Why I had this unique portal to the other side, I don't really know. As I grew, I learned that no one else could see what I saw and that therefore I had to cope with the secret of living with ghosts. That's not so easy when you're a little kid and want to be like everyone else. There were many times when I had to reconcile what I saw with what I was told about the unseen world. I soon realized that people's beliefs about ghosts and life after death were pretty scary stuff. It took me a while to differentiate my own feelings from the feelings of the ghosts around me. Like people, some ghosts were scary and some were nice. For the most part, the unseen strangers who came into my life ultimately changed it forever in a positive way.

So why are there ghosts in the first place? Do all ghosts haunt the living? Are there good ghosts and bad ghosts? And what can we do with all this information?

The journey beyond this earth is one of incredible beauty and creativity. Only those of us who are afraid choose to stay behind and cling to this earthly atmosphere. These earthbound ghosts are the kind written about in ghost stories and seen in scary movies. Not all ghosts are scary, yet the more knowledge we have, the more we can protect ourselves from those earthbound ghosts who want to encroach on our physical environment. These ghosts can be a negative influence on us, cause us to do things we might not otherwise do, and keep us locked in a world of fear and woe. On the other hand, there are spirits who can guide us to do the right thing and to pursue our dreams and who encourage us, thus making a positive difference in our lives. We can become aware of ghosts' energy by understanding our own. We can sense ghosts by using our intuitive mind, and we can tune in to the spirit forces around us to gain a proper perspective of ourselves in the world.

Use this book as a guide. There are plenty of examples of how ghosts have influenced my life and the lives of others. There are techniques, meditations, and various ways to contact ghosts and to know when ghosts have entered your life.

Before you take your fist step, however, look around at the world you know. When you finish reading this book, that world will never seem the same again.

ONE

Growing Up with Ghosts

"I see dead people." Those four words from *The Sixth Sense* have woven their way into popular culture and will forever be synonymous with a person describing his ability to see and communicate with ghosts. Since this highly successful film was released in 1999, a whole slew of books, movies, and TV shows have been created, most of which would have never seen the light of day a decade ago. No one seems impervious to a ghostly encounter or two anymore. In fact, people come up to me all the time to describe their own often incredible stories of ghostly apparitions. I am extremely thankful that I have been a part of educating others about spirit communication and life after death.

To begin on this journey of discovery, I first want to assure everyone that there is no such thing as death. Death refers only to the end of the physical body. I say this with surety because since the age of two I have been communicating with "the dead." Ghosts walk among us, impressing us with their love, guiding us with their wisdom, and protecting us from harm.

THE LOVE OF A GRANDFATHER

I will never forget the very first time I became aware of the others from a different world. I was a toddler in my crib, and I heard the sound of adult laughter coming from another room. I wanted so much to be out of the crib and with my parents. Like many babies, I cried for attention. My mother came into my room, picked me up, and soothed me for a while, then left me alone again. She didn't understand that I wanted to be with her and the rest of the adults in that other room. Night after night, I would stay awake and listen to the adults.

After a while, I became aware of tiny, sparkling lights dancing around my room, making unique patterns on the wall and around my crib. These sparkling lights fascinated me. Then one night the lights came together and formed a shape. I could see the shadow of a man standing in the corner of the room, his bright blue eyes piercing the darkness. He had a glow about him, a glow that came from inside out. I felt his presence to be very calming and loving. As he came closer to my crib, he smiled. There was nothing to be afraid of; in fact, he looked familiar to me. Although he never said anything, I could understand this man's thoughts. After his initial appearance, this ghost would occasionally visit and send me telepathic thoughts about painted ponies trotting around a ring of colorful shapes. I understood his thoughts because they were in the form of pictures, and I always felt a lot of light and love from him. As I grew older, his ghostly visits stopped.

By the time I was ready to start kindergarten, I would often spend weekends visiting my grandmother. The two of us shared a very special bond, and our visits were always filled with laughter and good food. On one of my trips to Grandma's apartment, I took out a family photo album. She sat next to me and told me about the people in the photos. When I saw the picture of the man with the bright blue eyes, standing in front of a tree, I pointed at it and asked, "Who's that?"

"He's your grandfather," she said. "He died before you were born. He came from England and went to work for the rodeo. You know, he even got a job setting up tents for the Buffalo Bill Wild West Show."

"I know him, Grandma. He used to visit me when I was a baby and tell me stories about the horses."

My grandmother smiled. I knew she didn't believe me. She merely added, "He loved telling stories about cowboys and Indians."

Years later, when I had begun my work as a medium, I remember finishing a reading and turning off my tape recorder. From the corner of my room, I heard a ghost say, *Good boy, James. I'm proud of you, son!* The kindly tone triggered the long-ago memory of the man with the bright blue eyes. I knew it was my grandfather. It was reassuring to know that he was still around watching over me.

A CHILD'S SENSITIVITY

My ghostly visitations had become a special part of my life, but unlike the boy in *The Sixth Sense*, I was never afraid of seeing or hearing ghosts, because they appeared to me as orbs of light. It all seemed so natural to me, as if everyone could see what I could see.

However, I was a sensitive child. I remember being terribly shy, and I didn't say much to anyone besides my mother and siblings. Other than seeing ghosts, I spent a fairly normal childhood. I lived in a small house in a family neighborhood of Bayside, Queens. The block was always filled with kids outside playing kickball or riding bikes. As I grew older, my shyness faded away, and I became more talkative and outgoing. However, I was always acutely aware of other people and could sense how they would act before they did. I could also tell when someone was truthful and trustworthy or when someone was deceitful and insincere. I was never really close to any of my schoolmates; even my best friend didn't know I could see ghosts. Sometimes I felt like a stranger in a strange land. I realized that I was different and had to accept that fact.

It seemed that the only ones I trusted were the ghosts. They were always friendly and interested in my welfare. I looked forward to communicating with these beings because they were the only ones who truly knew who I was. They were my real friends, and I felt extremely safe having them around. My mother was the only human to whom I confided. She knew about my secret life with ghosts. Fearing for my well-being, she would warn me, "Jamie, don't ever tell anybody what you see. They won't understand what you're talking about. You're different from other children." It just so happened that my mother was also different. She was extremely psychic and had the knack of predicting events before they happened. Sometimes I would pass her room and catch her in conversation with her deceased mother and father. I know because I could see their ghostly figures standing at the foot of her bed.

GHOSTS HAUNT THE CHURCH

Like many Catholic children in my neighborhood, I went to Sacred Heart Catholic School. My mother and I attended Mass every Sunday. We loved to sit in the balcony with the choir because we had a bird's-eye view of all the people in the pews and the priest up on the altar. The only thing that truly frightened me was the fifteen-foot crucifix with poor Jesus nailed to it. I used to wonder, why would people depict God suffering like that? I admit that I didn't always understand what was going on and wasn't really interested. However, I did enjoy the singing and the smell of incense. At that time, Mass was said in Latin. Usually, I would nod off into an altered state of consciousness as the priest droned on in a language I couldn't understand. I would see a myriad of ghosts milling about the aisles of the church. Some knelt in front of statues, others followed the priest at the altar, but mostly the ghosts stood alongside the churchgoers. Looking down from the balcony, I could see deceased parents around their children sharing Mass with them. I could see many child ghosts running around, playing with the hair or clothing of the living children. Some of the living children were aware of the ghosts and would play along. Sometimes a child would be frightened and let out a scream, and a parent would turn and scold him or her to be quiet. It all seemed like a fun game to me.

On other occasions, I could see ghosts kneeling in front of the statues of Mary, Jesus, or one of the saints. I used to ask my mother, "Why do they need to come to church and pray to the statues? Don't they see the real Mary and Jesus in heaven?" My mother would answer me, "Some people have old habits that make them feel good."

Generally speaking, a church is a vortex of spiritual energy, no matter the faith or denomination. People come together as a group to worship, contemplate, and pray in the name of God. These actions energize the spirit world, and ghosts show up to influence us with their love and guidance. It is no wonder that church is a place in which people find a safe haven.

I have a vivid recollection of one particular Sunday when the priest at the altar was holding the Host (the thin, round wafer that represents the body of Christ) above his head in consecration. He repeated a prayer in Latin, and everyone answered. It was at that moment that I saw several illuminated spirits dressed in white robes walk through the wall of the tabernacle. I knew they were special ghosts from heaven because I could feel a sense of adoration and reverence. Feeling so moved, I said out loud, "Mom, look at those men in white on the altar. Are they angels?" Everyone in the balcony turned in my direction. My mother's wide-eyed, stern gaze said it all. I knew I'd better keep my mouth shut before I got deeper into trouble. I certainly didn't want to upset my mother any more than I already had. However, I will always remember that beautiful sight. Seeing those heavenly messengers has proven to be one of the many sources of inspiration I have had along this wonderful journey.

THE LADY IN PINK

A year after I made my first communion, I was at Sunday Mass with my class. We all sat in the front pews of the church. Back then, before we could receive communion, we had to fast. Toward the middle of Mass, before the Lord's Prayer, I felt an intense pain in my stomach. I thought it was my poor empty belly crying out for food. The pain was so intense that I had to lie on the floor between the seat and the kneeler. The voice of the priest faded into the background, and I could feel the back of my neck getting wet with sweat. I wished someone could help me, but I was too afraid of being reprimanded by the nuns for acting weird, so I just stayed put. After a while, I was in my own little world. Suddenly I looked up, and a beautiful lady in a pink dress, with red hair, blue eyes, and the softest skin I had ever seen, bent over me. I looked into her eyes and heard her clearly through the din of the Mass.

Don't worry about what others think, James. You should never feel embarrassed to be who you are. As I help you today, one day you will help others in the same way. You will bring others peace. Love yourself, and all will be well.

I awakened from my trancelike state and managed to maneuver myself so that I could lean against the pew. By then, the priest was reciting the closing prayers. I was able to sit upright and look around. The lady in pink had vanished. As I peeked over at the other children, I was aware that no one wanted to make eye contact with me. *What could they be thinking?* I wondered. I kept my mouth shut because I was still a little dazed and confused about the lady in pink. It wasn't until many years later that I understood her message. It was one of many messages I had received by then from ghosts about bringing peace, hope, and love to others.

A GHOSTLY RESCUE

Because I was a shy, sensitive young man, I didn't have many friends. I wasn't into sports, nor was I the class clown. I was friendly enough, but not to everyone, and especially not to the school's troublemakers. These kids just seemed so ridiculous to me. They were always vying for attention from anyone and everyone.

When I was in fifth grade, Mike Marks was the class bully. Mike always sat in the back of the room so that he could make disturbing noises to ruin the class's concentration. He had a quick temper and a mean streak that was difficult to control. Our history teacher, Mr. Reed, was usually a calm man. He was articulate and smart and always seemed to make history come alive. One day Mike drove Mr. Reed to his boiling point. Mr. Reed called Mike to the front of the class and hit him over and over with his pointer. It was hard to watch Mike get a whipping, even if he deserved one. Then I saw the ghost. Like many of my visions, this ghost had a luminous light around him. It was a tall male figure, with brown hair and dark, swarthy features. He stood to the right of Mike and sadly watched Mike getting a licking. At one point, the ghost brought his hands up to his face to shield the horrible scene from his eyes. I realized that the ghost was Mike's father, and he wanted to tell Mike how sorry he was. I wished I could have relayed the message to Mike, but at the time that was impossible. I felt sorry for Mike. I had always thought that the poor guy was probably beaten by his father and that was why he acted the way he did. Perhaps his outbursts were a cry for help. Outside of the classroom, I saw Mike only at Cub Scout meetings. He was just as loud and obnoxious there as he was in school.

One day on my way home from school, Mike was behind me, walking in the same direction. He caught up with me and asked if he could join me. I only agreed because I thought it was cool to hang out with the big bully. He suggested that we go by the train trestle.

"It's out of my way," I said timidly.

Mike picked up a rock and aimed it at my head. I was petrified. In a threatening tone, he said, "Do what I say, or I'll crack your head open."

I walked with Mike a good forty-five minutes to the train trestle. It was in the most out-of-the-way location next to the Clearview Expressway. No one was around because no one would have a reason to be there. By then, Mike had already thrown down the rock, so I figured he was goofing with me. When we arrived at the trestle, Mike told me to sit down and take off my sneakers.

"C'mon, Mike," I said. "The joke's over. I'm going home."

Mike got angry again. "Do it, or I'll beat you up."

I quickly untied my shoes and handed them to Mike.

Holding my shoes over the expressway, Mike said, "Tell me I'm great, or I'll fling them over."

I didn't know which was worse—getting beat up by Mike or getting punished by my father for losing my sneakers. I thought Mike was crazy, and I just wanted to get away from him. I started to run away, but Mike grabbed me and threw me down. My hands and face hit the ground hard.

I began to plead. "Why are you doing this?"

"Because I can. Don't you know I'm great?"

I started to run again. This time when Mike caught me, he held me over the zooming afternoon traffic. I was scared to death; he was crazy enough to drop me.

"Put me down!" I screamed.

Mike just laughed.

Suddenly the ghost I had seen standing next to Mike in the classroom returned. He looked the same, only this time he seemed to be brighter. The ghost sent me his thoughts.

I am Michael, Mike's dad.

"Your father is talking to me," I said to Mike.

"What are you talking about?" Mike yelled back.

"Your father is here with us."

Mike put me down on the ground and looked at me like I was the crazy one.

"Your father is saying that it was not your fault. He was drunk and got into a car accident."

Mike stared at me.

"He says he was supposed to go to your Little League game, but he didn't show up because he died the night before."

"That's not true," Mike insisted. "My mother said he left us."

Mike's father told me that his wife lied because she felt too guilty about having an affair. She had asked Mike's father for a divorce the day he died.

"Don't blame yourself," I said. "It wasn't your fault. He says he is very proud of you, and he's sorry that you didn't know the real story about his death."

Mike threw my sneakers at me and ran away. The ghost thanked me for telling his son the truth.

I felt sorry for the ghost, but thanked him for saving my life.

Mike never spoke to me again. I learned from my mother that Mike's father did die in an auto accident. A year after that incident, Mike disappeared from the neighborhood. I later heard he went to military school in upstate New York.

STARTING OVER

The older I grew, the less interest I had in ghosts. I spent a year in a high school preparatory seminary and realized that although I was searching for the answers, the Catholic Church wasn't the place I would find them. When I entered public high school, I was too wrapped up in being a teenager to deal with the other side. I was still very intuitive, but I sort of closed the portal to my visions. By then, I had entered San Francisco State College and was majoring in broadcasting. I wanted to pursue a career as a TV comedy writer.

After college, I moved to L.A., where I got a lot of odd jobs in the film business to learn what it was all about. One day Carol, a friend from the office, asked me to go with her to a séance. I wasn't sure that I wanted to start this whole business with ghosts again, but I went, mostly out of curiosity. There I met Brian E. Hurst, a gifted and popular medium. At one point in the séance, Brian turned to me and said, "The spirits tell me that you are a gifted medium and one day will be doing this work too."

I thought to myself, *No way! I'm not this crazy. I'm going to be a TV writer, not someone who speaks to the dead.* However, my interest was piqued, and I kept going back to Brian's weekly séances.

Eventually, I began to see ghosts again, just like when I was a kid. So I started doing my own individual readings, first with friends and then with referrals. After a year, the readings had become a full-time job, and I had to make a choice. Was I going to quit readings to pursue TV, or was I going to quit TV to pursue communication with ghosts? Needless to say, I quit my day job in show business and became a full-time medium. That was almost twenty-five years ago, and it has been a wild ride ever since.

Having traveled around the world, I can say without a doubt that ghosts are among us everywhere.

T W O

Leaving the Body

In my field of work, I am constantly asked the same questions over and over. What is it like to die? Is there really an afterlife, and if so, where do we go? Is there any pain?

Death is the great unknown. By the time our end draws near, we have developed so many preconceived notions about death and dying through religious and societal beliefs that we have no true understanding of the event. Even though each person's death experience is an individual one, based on my communication with spirits, I can tell you that there are some incredible similarities in making the transition.

- No matter what factors are present at death—homicide, suicide, explosion, accident, old age—there is one constant that remains. There is *no pain* when you die. I can never say this enough to people. In fact, it is this absence of pain that confuses many of the newly dead because they do not realize that they have died.

- No one ever dies alone. When we pass out of our bodies, deceased loved ones are always there to greet us. We may not have seen these people for many years, but the love bonds we experienced on earth are still very much continued on the other side.

- Many experience a sense of being surrounded by a brilliant light and being pulled through a tunnel. People describe the light as God, or an all-knowing being. Some feel that the light is pure peace, joy, and love. Instead of a light, some ghosts describe being surrounded by a glorious display of celestial colors like nothing they have ever seen.

- There is an immediate sense of not being limited to the physical body. The life once lived simply falls away. In its place is an awareness of a "newness" to life.

- Finally, when we stand at the doorway to death, there seems to be an immediate altering of time and space. Ghosts are in a timeless, ethereal, transparent dimension. Earth time may be passing, but to a ghost everything is happening *now*.

NO PAIN

Why do we escape pain at the very end? Can our spirits be aware of our impending demise and therefore shut down our pain receptors just before we die? It seems as if the Universe has indeed provided some sort of shutoff valve in our brains that goes into effect just before we leave our bodies. A person enters a blackout period and loses consciousness and memory. When I ask spirits about the violence of an accident, or about a bullet entering their flesh, or about their death by heart attack, they often respond that they don't remember the impact of the disaster. Instead, their first memories are of their loved ones. In one way or another, each has said, "I wish my [wife, husband, mother, father, daughter, sister, brother, son] knew that I was still alive."

That was the case with a young male ghost who appeared in one of my New York workshops.

"This is a young man about seventeen or eighteen who gives me the name of Sam and tells me he was crushed in a car."

A woman named Debbie jumped out of her seat. "Oh, my God, that's Sam. That's my Sam," she shouted.

"He wants me to tell you not to cry for him. He is saying that he is alive and fine."

Debbie held tissues up to her nose as she nodded up and down.

"He wants you to know that his body flew out of the front window."

She nodded again, and I continued.

"He is telling me to let you and everyone else in the audience know that he was unaware of himself going through the window. He doesn't remember it, and he didn't feel any pain. He saw his body afterward by the tree, and that's when he realized what had happened."

"Okay, I understand," said Debbie.

"He says he is with Alfred. Alfred helped him."

Debbie continued her crying. "Alfred is my father. I knew he would be there for Sam."

"He is telling me that he blacked out before the impact, and then he saw his grandfather. He thought he was dreaming, but his grandfather told him that he was in an accident. He had Sam look at his body."

Then something odd came to me. "Sam is showing me his body. I am seeing his left leg in an odd position. Do you know if his left leg was broken or torn from his body?"

"Yes," Debbie replied. "It was broken in seven places along with various ribs."

"Your son wants me to tell you that when he looked down at his body, he felt that it wasn't his anymore. He didn't feel connected to it. He felt as though he were out of it and didn't need it anymore. He also knows about the rocks you set up at the accident scene to commemorate his life. He loved the gesture very much and wants you to know that."

Debbie looked shocked. "I just did that this week. Can I ask you something? Can Sam hear me?"

"Yes. He is able to hear all of your thoughts all of the time. He knows when you are thinking of him."

The reading continued with more details about Sam's passing. Then Debbie's father, Alfred, spoke a little.

"Alfred is saying, don't worry. Daddy is taking care of everything."

Debbie seemed extremely grateful and pleased.

NEAR-DEATH EXPERIENCE

Those who have touched death and come back to tell about it seem to share a multitude of similarities. Although these people come from all walks of life, have different religious beliefs, and vary in age from children to seniors, they tell a variation of the same story.

- A sensation of floating above one's body and seeing the surrounding area

- Pleasant feelings of calmness and overwhelming peace

- Moving through a tunnel or narrow passageway of light

- Being greeted by deceased relatives

- Encounters with an angel, a being of light, or a religious figure

- Experiencing a life review

- Reaching a border or boundary that one cannot cross

- Finally, a feeling of rapidly moving back into one's body, often with great reluctance

Although every person's situation is different, all of them agree that their lives have been profoundly changed by their near-death experience. Most come to understand their life's purpose, and many share insights about the lessons they have had to learn. In fact, they are downright adamant that if it had not been for the near-death experience, they would be living a very different life.

A woman at one of my workshops told me that she was always afraid to try something new. When she had a heart attack at the age of sixty and went through the tunnel toward the light, she was met by her nephew, who had committed suicide because of his schizophrenia.

"He looked so calm and happy. It had been a long time since I had seen him at peace."

Her nephew told her that she should try to live her life more spontaneously, and then he disappeared.

"That experience changed me. If my nephew, who had suffered so much in his life, came to tell me to live life more fully, I decided that I would do just that. It was my way of showing him that he was my inspiration. Since that time, I have traveled more and have had friends stay over at my home whenever they are in town, both things I was afraid of doing. My life is more enjoyable because I have seen death and I've decided to live."

MY NEAR-DEATH EXPERIENCE

Since people had often shared their near-death experiences with me, I was particularly curious. I wondered if their reference points about the afterlife were the same as the ones I had received from the spirit world. On December 10, 2006, I got my answer.

The holiday season was in full swing. While people circled around parking lots and spilled into shopping malls in search of the perfect whatever for whomever, I stood on my deck, cup of coffee in hand, and gazed at the panoramic view of the glistening blue Pacific Ocean before me. I felt blessed just to be alive. Regrettably, the blaring ring of the telephone interrupted my reverie. It was my manager, Andrew Lear. He had made an appointment for me in L.A. with the head of a radio station about doing my own radio show. Reluctant to leave my peaceful surroundings, I waved good-bye to the billowy clouds and rushed inside to take a shower. I had just enough time to make it to L.A. by lunch . . . if I was lucky.

As I crawled my way up the 405 freeway in the middle of a beautiful morning, I fantasized about how great it would be when we could think about a place and be there without having to deal with any type of traffic. By the time I finally reached my destination, it was past lunchtime, and I was starving. I pulled into the first strip center I could find and headed for the nearest sandwich shop. My meeting was to start in five minutes, so I stood next to my car and wolfed down my turkey, lettuce, and tomato sandwich as quickly as I could.

Fortunately, my meeting went well, even though my stomach suffered from the aftereffects of my lunch. I happily agreed to create a pilot of an on-air, live-audience demonstration of talking to the dead. After the meeting ended, I headed to the parking lot, not looking forward to the long, tiresome return trip to Orange County. Fortunately, my friend Victoria Recano called and invited me to dinner. "I'm so glad you called," I said to Victoria. "The thought of another two and a half hours in the car . . ."

The two of us met for dinner in Beverly Hills at Wolfgang Puck's trendy new restaurant, CUT. Victoria and I had struck up a friendship while shooting my five-minute segments for *Enter-tainment Tonight*'s "The Insider" show. We both were in the mood for steak, so we ordered identical dinners topped off by a delicious red wine. After dinner, I headed for my part-time apartment across from CBS Studios. It was my home away from home when *The Ghost Whisperer* was in production.

In the middle of the night, I was unexpectedly awakened by an intense ache in my stomach and had just enough time to make it to the bathroom. The dinner I had so enjoyed just a few hours before stared back at me from the bathroom sink. *It had to be a reaction to the wine,* I thought, as I climbed back into bed and tried to go back to sleep. However, it was not meant to be. For the next several hours, I was in and out of the bathroom until I was too tired to move. By six in the morning, I had decided that I would feel better if I was in my own home, snug in my own bed. With all the strength I could muster, I got dressed and got on the road again. I thought my nightmare would soon come to an end when I reached the safety of my home. However, halfway there, the traffic on the freeway came to a dead stop. All I could see was an unending sea of red taillights. Several hours and a dozen restroom stops later, I exited the freeway and finally reached my destination. I immediately phoned my Los Angeles doctor, who also happened to be a friend, and told her my problem.

In her matter-of-fact tone, she said, "Honey, you have food poisoning. Come into the office, and I'll give you something for it."

"No! I can't!" I practically screamed. "I'm already back home in Laguna. I can't even hold my head up." (I am sure that those of you who have had the unfortunate experience of food poisoning can empathize with my outburst.)

"Stay in bed and drink plenty of fluids and get some Gatorade. I'll call in a prescription for an anti-nausea medication."

"Do you think I should go to the emergency room?"

"I don't think it's necessary. They would probably give you the same medication. Just drink fluids and take the medication. Don't worry, you'll feel better soon. I'll check with you in the morning."

I hung up and suddenly thought of my dinner companion, Victoria. I called her to see if she was okay.

"I feel fine," she said with a sympathetic tone in her voice. "Did you have anything else to eat yesterday?"

Suddenly I zeroed in on my sandwich. "Yes!" I shouted. "It must have been the sandwich."

"It could have been unwashed lettuce," Victoria suggested. "I hope you feel better."

Several hours later, my good friend Brian came over to take care of me. The anti-nausea medicine didn't seem to be working, so I decided to give my doctor another call.

"It's a bad case of food poisoning. Just keep drinking fluids."

By eleven o'clock that evening, I was weaker than ever from vomiting all night long. No matter what, I had to get to the hospital. I managed to get up off the couch and walk into the bathroom. The last thing I remember seeing was the bathroom sink.

Suddenly I felt that I was floating out of my body. I felt connected to my body, but not necessarily in it. At first, I could see the top of my head, and the next thing I knew I could see my body on the bathroom floor. A rush of thoughts and emotions flooded through me, and I felt as if I were dying. The most vivid memory was of how much better I felt. No more pain, no more vomiting. Before I knew it, a luminous, golden light seemed to fill the space around me. I could hear someone say to me, *Dying is easy. Living is hard.* Instantly, I was aware of my dead cousin Pat. Pat was my favorite and closest cousin growing up, and we used to spend hours talking about life after death and the idea of reincarnation. In a way, she was the first person I ever spoke to about spiritual matters, and we both shared a mistrust for Catholicism. Pat died when I was nineteen; I was heartbroken. I had never seen her as a ghost until that moment. She stared at me with her smiling eyes. She looked so young and pretty in her blue-green satin top.

Pat whispered, *Don't worry, it will be all over soon.*

I mentally asked her, *Do you mean* over *over? Or just* over?

At that point, Pat disappeared, and I was aware of my father's presence. He stood in the distance, wearing a brown sweater. He too appeared to be a younger version of himself. Suddenly I heard a swooshing sound and Brian's voice.

"James, wake up. Are you okay?"

I opened my eyes and looked around. I felt calm, yet at a loss for words. Then I said, "Dying is easy. Living is hard."

"Okay, I'm calling 911," Brian said without missing a beat. By the time I got to the ER, I had been in and out of consciousness several times. I was told that I had lost five pints of fluid and blood and needed a blood transfusion. All that vomiting had caused a tear in my esophagus, I was hemorrhaging internally, and I had E-coli poisoning from the food I had eaten.

To say the least, I was glad to be alive because I knew I still had work to do. Having my own near-death experience cemented my faith in my spiritual communication. Going through the dying experience showed me that there was nothing else left to be afraid of.

COMA

I am often asked, "Can people in comas hear us?" Even when an individual appears to be physically unresponsive or in a vegetative state, he or she may not be completely unaware of what is happening. That person may also not be aware *all the time*, because I also believe there are various degrees of a "coma" state of mind. However, consciousness is always aware of what's going on.

There are many levels of consciousness: (1) waking conscious-ness; (2) automatic consciousness, which keeps our blood flow-ing, cells dividing, and so forth; and (3) higher consciousness, which occurs in deep relaxation, meditation, prayer, dreaming, and daydreaming. I believe that my communication with ghosts is part of this higher consciousness. Simply put, consciousness is awareness of all of our internal and external experiences. To me it is the "*all*." Consciousness is not confined to the body; it is a part of the mind, and the mind is a part of the soul. At the time of death, the soul, which is eternal and contains experiences from eons of lifetimes, moves on.

My father was bedridden in a hospital for the last two weeks of his life. In a coma, he was hooked up to machines, respirators, and IVs. It was a situation that he would never have wanted. On his final night, his doctors called and told my family that Dad did not have much longer to live. When we arrived at the hospital, we filed into his room, one by one, to say our good-byes. I was the last one. Throughout that last two-week period, I had noticed his dead parents and my deceased mother lingering in his room. That particular night, my mother seemed quite impatient; she kept saying, *Hurry up and say your good-byes already. We want him with us!*

My brother and sisters were standing around watching my father in his last moments of life. I approached his bed, bent down, and whispered in his ear, "It's time for you to go home. Go toward the brilliant light that you see."

I heard him respond to me from about two feet above my head, as if he were watching the whole thing. I knew that he would be completely aware of what was happening because he knew by then that it was time for him to go. He spoke telepathi-cally to me in a very clear and very firm tone, and he asked me to grant his final wish. *I just don't want you kids fighting when I leave.*

I promised, *We won't, Dad*, and kissed him on his head. *Enjoy your journey home.*

When we left the room, I repeated Dad's words to my siblings. Everyone chuckled. My brother-in-law, Jay, jokingly added, "I guess we'd better change our phone numbers then."

Within five minutes of our last good-byes, Dad died. The doctor seemed surprised; he had given Dad at least another day or so. I turned to the doctor and told him, "He wanted to leave. His whole family was waiting for him."

The doctor grinned, turned, and walked away.

GHOSTS ATTEND THEIR FUNERALS

After the dead leave their physical body and realize that they are no longer attached to their body, they move into the membrane between earth and the next dimension closest to earth. At this time, ghosts make up their mind whether they want to remain close to the earth as earthbound ghosts or cross into the light. During this window of opportunity, ghosts usually attend their funeral to see how they are being laid out, who shows up, the various preparations, and so on. I have heard many odd remarks by ghosts while attending their funeral. *Why did they put that dress on me? Who picked those flowers for my casket? I want to be in a bronze urn, not a wooden box.* Often I have heard ghosts say that they do not like having an open casket. Some male ghosts have communicated that they do not like being "made up" for their funeral. Many a ghost has caused plenty of havoc at his or her funeral in order to help the loved ones "get it right." Then there are those who don't give a second thought to the details of their funeral and are very surprised by all the fuss being made over them.

When my father died, my siblings and I scoured the attic for old photographs to set around the funeral parlor for his wake. He must have been quite impressed because, as I was catching up with an old school chum after the memorial service, I felt a cold breeze behind me. It was Dad. He whispered in my ear, *Where did you find all those old photos of me? I don't even remember taking them.* Then he added, *Thanks for putting my teeth back in. I look pretty good.*

It is also common for ghosts to attend their autopsy. No longer attached to their physical body, they want to see how they died or what caused their death. If they died of a certain disease, they may want to see how the disease killed them. To us, these ideas may seem morbid, but that is because we are still mentally attached to our bodies. I think the HBO series *Six Feet Under* perfectly captures the life of the newly dead. The dead see their bodies as old, worn-out coats that they no longer need. I cannot tell you how many times I have had a spirit say to a loved one, *Why do you go to the grave and stare at the dirt? I'm not in there.*

For years my cousin Ruth, sister Lynn, Aunt Cassie, and I would talk about life after death. It seemed that the work I was doing fascinated them. We would often share memories of our dead relatives. I come from a big Irish family on my mother's side, and I spent a lot of time in my childhood attending funerals. Seeing dead bodies in coffins was quite common to me. I remember how much Aunt Cassie would obsess over relatives who had passed, always remembering their death anniversaries, keeping their obituaries and the funeral sermons pasted in a scrapbook. We would often joke together over the telephone. She used to say to me, "If there's an afterlife, I am going to make sure to scare the bugaboos out of you!"

Aunt Cassie passed away in her late eighties. She literally sat down in her living room chair and died. Because she was the last of her generation to leave, all of her nieces and nephews showed up for her funeral. It was a wake like no other. As I sat with my back against a wall, talking to my sister Lynn and cousin Ruth, I joked, "You know, Cassie will have to make an appearance." Suddenly all three of us felt an icy-cold chill run through our veins. We looked at each other in amazement. I glanced upward and saw Aunt Cassie standing there with my mother and the rest of my aunts and uncles. Cassie was pointing at us and laughing. She wore a white dress with a green print. She looked stunningly young, and quite different from the stiff body laid out in the coffin. I heard her saying to me, *What? Did you think I would miss my own funeral?*

I shared my vision with Lynn and Ruth. My cousin looked at me and remarked, "You are so weird!" The three of us shared a laugh. We were happy that Cassie was finally back home with the family she had missed so much and had wanted to be with for such a long time.

After the funeral, what's next for ghosts? It depends on a number of factors. Was death the result of a prolonged illness? Did the person have strong religious beliefs? Was the person afraid of dying? Was the person in an accident or murdered? Was the person a child? Because our consciousness doesn't die at death, we carry our mind-set of thoughts and beliefs with us to the other side. As in life, so in death. When we cross over into the other dimensions, we continue to create experiences through our thoughts, the same way we did in life.

ENTERING THE LIGHT

The newly dead are usually drawn to a brilliant white light. What exactly is this white light, and why do most sense it at the time of death? Scientifically, when all colors come together as one, they become white. I believe that this white light is at one end of the dimensional spectrum and blends all colors of the light spectrum. I believe that this "end of colors" is the threshold to another dimension, and it's interesting that the song "Somewhere Over the Rainbow" seems to refer to it exactly. The other side of the rainbow is the end of the spectrum of color as we know it. Perhaps that is why this song strikes a chord with so many people and is still so popular more than a half century after it was written.

When I was a child, I had a vision of this white light and thought of it as the hand of God. It was a feeling of joy and pure unconditional love. It seems to be the same for those who have had near-death experiences. They are drawn to this luminous light and feel utter peace as they go toward it. Like me, some have characterized the light as God, while others, with no particular philosophy, have called it the "all-knowing" or "home."

Suffice it to say that the white light is indeed a doorway or a portal, and once you go through it, you have entered the spiritual dimensions and arrived home. Not once when doing my work have spirits ever said to me that they wished they could come back to earth and live again. The spirits with whom I communicate are usually thrilled that they are in the light and would want it no other way. Their biggest regrets have to do with not realizing the truth about life when they were alive on earth. They often comment that, had they known, their lives would have been very different.

BLUE THUNDER

I find it fascinating to listen to various ghosts discuss how they experience the other side. For one thing, they seem to have an overwhelming sense of being free. When they realize they have passed over, they immediately go to their grieving family members and attempt to tell them that there is no need to be sad because they are still very much alive. Also, it seems that they enter a world that perfectly fits their level of spiritual understanding.

A couple of years ago, a dear friend called and asked if I could see Candy, a young woman whom she thought was at her breaking point. "You are her last resort, James." I agreed to see her.

When Candy arrived for her appointment, I ushered her into my living room. Candy had long, blond hair that framed her beautiful high cheekbones and green eyes. She seemed anxious, so I offered to get her a glass of water. "Take some deep breaths and relax," I suggested as I left the room.

Returning with the water, I assured Candy, "You're safe here." As she sat on a chair catching her breath, I explained how the process of spirit communication worked and began a brief meditation in order to relax her and release any nervousness. In the middle of the meditation, I saw two men standing behind her, one young and one older.

"There's an older gentleman behind you. I feel it is a father figure. He is mentioning something about being from Scotland and has a slight Scottish accent. He has a black-and-white sheepdog named Sharkey."

Candy seemed to be in shock and glared at me, desperately trying to understand how I could know such things.

Then she broke down and wept. "Yes. That is my father, Alex. He was Scottish and very proud of his heritage. Sharkey was our family dog, whom he loved even more than us kids."

"He says to give love to your mom."

Candy said through tearful eyes, "Mom misses Dad very much."

Even though this was an amazing connection, I still felt there was something more important coming.

"I'm picking up a young man with your father who keeps on talking about 'Blue Thunder.' Your father wants you to know that he helped this young man cross over."

Candy was dumbfounded and sobbed even more.

"He says his name is David," I said. "He is dressed all in white and is showing me a wedding ceremony. He seems to be somewhere tropical like Hawaii."

Then it dawned on me. I looked at Candy and said, "This is your fiancé, isn't it?"

"Yes."

"I feel that David is extremely sorry for being so pushy about Blue Thunder. Does that make sense?"

Candy nodded her understanding.

Then, in my mind's eye, I saw a car with the number "64" on its side spinning around in flames.

Candy was amazed at my revelation. "David was a professional race car driver. We were supposed to go to Hawaii and get married and then go around the world for our honeymoon. David liked meeting new people and experiencing different cultures. He insisted on finishing one more race before Hawaii. He was fine until the final lap, when he lost control, and his car, Blue Thunder, number sixty-four, exploded into flames, and he died."

I was stunned. Both of us sat silently, letting it all sink in.

Then I resumed my communication with David. "He tells me July is a special month."

"We were going to get married in July."

"Are you planning on still going? He is telling me that you and he had been to Hawaii to pick out a special place."

"Yes, I'm thinking of going back there to scatter his ashes."

Suddenly I was transfixed as David took control of my thoughts and vision. "He shows me that he was unaware of the accident. He remembers looking up at the crowd and seeing your face. Next to you, he saw your dead dad, and the next thing he knew he was out of the car, although he doesn't remember leaving it. Your father told him he had a bad accident. He is saying he couldn't believe it. He thought it was all a nightmare. So he went to the wreckage to witness his remains. Then he went to you and tried to tell you that he wasn't dead and that he was standing right next to you, but you couldn't hear him. After a while, your father took him by the shoulder. At that point, he knew that everything was going to be all right. He became aware of a beautiful green field surrounded by mountains. He saw his grandparents,

Lib and Burt, whom he hadn't seen since his childhood, coming to greet him along with other people. He says he hadn't thought of these people in years. A friend, Tom, also came to see him. Tom had died in some kind of a military uprising. He is now taking me to an incredible lake surrounded by tropical trees, ginger plants, and gardenias."

Candy took in the entire picture.

"He says that heaven is more than he ever imagined it to be. It all seems so natural. He was shocked because he never really thought about life after death, but he is very happy to know it exists."

Candy told me, "That place you're describing sounds exactly like the place where we were going to get married."

"He'll be there waiting for you."

David kept talking. "He says he thinks he had to go the time he did in order for various events to occur in the future. He is also telling me that he is aware that there are other places to visit in the spirit world. It is not like heaven as one would think. It seems that there are different spheres where people who think alike reside. He is very excited to explore heaven. He is saying, it is all for the good. He thinks this may be hard for you to under-stand. He wants you to know he is telling the truth. One day you will hold his hand again, and you'll be together forever."

INSIGHTS FROM THE SPIRIT WORLD

I have gathered a lot of information over the years from my com-munication with spirits who have crossed over into the light. Here are further insights about life after death.

- No one ever dies alone. No matter what, there are always friends, family members, and others there to greet you. Often there are spirits from many lifetimes ago to meet you as well. Your soul recognizes all whom you have known.

- In the spirit world, there is no time as we know it. Past and future do not exist. All "time" is now.

- When you arrive on the other side, you have a life review. You witness and actively experience important moments in your recent life. You become aware of the soul lessons that you had to learn. Only you are the judge of yourself. Only you will know if you learned the lesson or not. No one else judges you. If you hurt someone on earth, you experience that exact same hurt. Only you can forgive yourself for the pain that you caused another soul, and only you can forgive yourself for the pain you caused yourself.

- You see clearly the importance of your life and its effect on others.

- You become aware of yourself on a soul level and understand the vastness of a multidimensional universe.

- Your consciousness expands. You understand how previous lifetimes influenced your judgment of the life you just lived.

- You realize that the spirit world is made up of thousands of levels and that spirits gravitate to particular levels depending on their soul's evolution.

- You know that Universal Law rules everything, and that like always attracts like.

- You learn that there are lower, darker levels for unevolved souls and those who have not yet learned to appreciate their lives or the lives of others.

- You realize that life never ends. Life continues forever in different forms and in different dimensions.

Let me just say that leaving your body at death is as natural as being born. It's like moving, only without all the bother of packing. You are moving to a new neighborhood, and it may take some getting used to, but you will be the same you when you arrive. With this in mind, you might be curious about what it means to become a ghost, what you will look and feel like, and where you will end up when you leave your body.

THREE

Ghosts 101

In a sense, we all are ghosts—that is, spirits residing in physical bodies. When our spiritual work is done on this earth, our physical bodies shut down and our ghostly body exits. The solid, dense energy of our physical body begins to deteriorate. The light, transparent energy body that is an exact replica of the physical body emerges and moves into the spirit worlds. There are no mistakes, and no deaths before their time. Nor are there deaths that could have been avoided. Why? Because there is no death, period. There is only a transition from a physical existence to a nonphysical one. Once we are on the other side, we are officially termed "ghosts." Ghosts are either "in the light" or "earthbound." Most of the ghosts with whom I communicate are in the light. Most scary ghost stories are about earthbound ghosts.

When most of us think about ghosts, we tend to clump them into the same category with werewolves, vampires, and zombies. Ghosts are not ghouls who roam graveyards at midnight looking to scare people out of their wits. This perception couldn't be farther from the truth. Granted, ghosts want to communicate with us, but mostly they want to help us, not scare us. That being said,

earthbound ghosts can scare us. Since they have not yet entered
the light, they are caught between the earth's dimension and the
spiritual realm. Earthbound ghosts are usually fearful, angry, or
lonely, and they communicate with these kinds of emotions.

Before we go on, let me explain exactly what a ghost is. Ac-
cording to the *Donning International Encyclopedic Psychic Dictionary*,
the definition of a ghost is

> an energy field that makes its presence known periodically
> in the same area, giving the awareness of a living person;
> brings a drop in temperature with its presence; perceived
> clairaudient or audiently by its activities and movements;
> perceived clairvoyantly as a fluffy, transparent human-like
> mass, moving very slowly . . .

Although this description is somewhat dramatic, it is not far
from the truth. Here is my definition of a ghost.

Ghosts are forms of energy, just as humans are forms of energy.
They appear quite like their physical bodies. When I see ghosts,
I rarely see fragments of a person, like a head or an arm, floating
around in space. I see neither a mass of swirling, white clouds nor
a white sheet with two holes cut out where eyes would supposedly
be. I always see full human forms, complete with hair, facial features, and clothing. Most of the time, ghosts appear youthful,
healthy, and in the prime of life.

However, in some instances, ghosts can appear exactly the way
they were at the time of death. When ghosts materialize in this
condition, death may have been sudden and unexpected, and they
may not be aware that they have passed from the physical world.

Temperatures do change when ghosts are around. Mostly the
air feels colder. Usually, I feel a cool breeze across the back of my
neck. Ghosts definitely are perceived clairvoyantly and clairaudi-
ently, but I have yet to hear a ghost shriek, *Boo!*

In addition, the physical laws of the universe do not limit ghosts. Therefore, time and gravity do not affect them. Without the dense energy of physical bodies to encapsulate them, ghost bodies vibrate at a rate we cannot measure.

Ghosts can travel from one place to another instantaneously because they live in an atmosphere solely created by their own thoughts and attitudes. So, whatever they imagine, that is where they are. It could be a palace, a dungeon, a field of flowers, or a void. It could be your house, my house, another planet, the subway, or the apartment they once lived in.

Also, ghosts are extremely sensitive, so they can pick up on your thoughts and feelings with crystal-clear clarity, as if they had some kind of special radar. Just thinking of a loved one who has passed over can attract that ghost to you.

A FATHER FINDS HIS WAY BACK HOME

I often do readings in demonstrations among hundreds and sometimes thousands of people. It gives me the opportunity to work with many different people all in one place, and the communication is often wonderful and inspiring. When a demonstration begins, ghosts line up behind me and around their loved ones in the audience, trying their best to get a message through to a husband, wife, relative, or friend. Often, in their communication, ghosts describe what it's like to die. They want to make sure people understand that death is a very natural process and not the end. Sometimes it takes a person a while to even realize that he or she is dead and is in ghostly form.

Several years back I was in Kansas doing one of my demonstrations. A forceful ghost immediately got my attention, and I made a connection with a young woman in the audience by the name of Annie. It was the ghost's daughter. I walked over to Annie and asked her to stand up.

"Your father is here."

"Really?" she said skeptically.

"He is telling me that he wasn't found for a couple of days."

"Oh, my God, that's him."

"He wants you to know that the last thing he remembers was checking the inventory. Do you understand?"

"Yes. He was a foreman at the Seward warehouse."

"Is his name George?"

"Yes," she said excitedly.

George was so happy to finally contact someone. "He says he wanted to make sure the inventory report got out in time before tax season."

"Yes, he was in charge of the inventory report. He worked long hours to prepare it."

"I see him climbing a ladder. He reaches over to some supplies all the way at the back of the shelf. He is trying to reach them, but he can't. He says he lost his balance and fell off the ladder. That's the last thing he remembers."

I asked George, *When did you know you were a ghost?*

George responded to me with his thoughts. *I didn't believe it was real. It was quite a strange thing, you know. I don't actually remember falling, but I knew I couldn't hold on. I remember being on the ladder, looking down at my body on the cement floor. I thought I was dreaming. How could I be on the floor and on the ladder at the same time? I was fine on the ladder. I felt like I had a week's worth of sleep. I looked down at my body on the floor and couldn't feel anything for that person. I tried to call for help, but there was no one in the warehouse except me. Then I began to panic. If I didn't get up off the floor, I was going to die or something. Then everything went kind of foggy.*

I looked at Annie. "Do you understand what he is talking about?"

Annie was very quiet. She seemed to be mesmerized by what I was saying.

George kept sending me his thoughts, and I conveyed them as best I could to his daughter.

"Standing in front of your father was his old service buddy. He is saying they served together in Vietnam."

I looked at Annie. "Do you know this person? Your father says his name is Marty."

Annie shook her head.

"He says that he hadn't seen Marty in forty years. He says that Marty was there to rescue him and to help him find his way back home. Your father doesn't understand why Marty was trying to help him. He says Marty reminded him that when they were in Vietnam he saved Marty from stepping on a land mine. Your dad is saying that he saved Marty, and now Marty was there to save him."

I could tell that people in the audience seemed to connect with George.

I continued. "Your father says that he saw the image of the jungle and the whole thing happening all over again as if they were right back in Nam. He is saying that it was very strange."

George was conveying a very moving image, and it touched most of the people in the audience. Many had tears in their eyes.

"Your father is saying that Marty couldn't save him from dying, but he wanted to help him move on. Your father still couldn't believe that he was dead."

I turned to Annie and smiled. "Your father is kind of stubborn, isn't he? He has to see it to believe it."

Annie nodded. "That's him."

"He says he asked Marty to take him to see you and your mother, Maggie, and instantly they were in your living room. He says the room was a terrible mess."

"We had called the police because he was gone for two days, and we didn't hear from him," Annie replied.

"Your father saw you and your husband, Steve, trying to comfort your mother."

Annie validated this to the audience. "That's right. We were waiting to hear from the police. Suddenly the doorbell rang, and two policemen stood in the doorway. They told us there was an accident in the warehouse."

"Your father was very confused. He knew he was standing next to you, yet no matter how much he tried to tell you he was all right, no one could see or feel him."

I asked George if anyone else besides Marty came to bring him into the light.

Well, I was in a bit of a state, and when I heard the cops say I was dead, I didn't know what to do. So in my head I asked for help, and before long I began seeing right through the front wall of my house. My younger brother Tommy appeared. He looked like a kid again. Then my grandmother came. She looked beautiful, like a young woman. Tommy told me that it was time to go home. I didn't know what he meant by that. I thought I was home. He said that our mother would come in a little while. So I went with Tommy and my grandmother, and that was it, really.

Annie asked, "Anyone else, Dad?"

"He's telling me . . . Clyde."

I couldn't tell whether Annie was going to cry or laugh. "Oh, Clyde . . . Clyde was the dog he had when he was a boy."

FUNNY GIRL

The following reading occurred during a demonstration in Florida. The room was filled with about seven hundred people. The ghost in this scenario did not remember any details of her passing, but once in the light, she felt very happy.

I started singing onstage because of this lady's exuberant energy. "Sadie . . . Sadie, married lady. I want to go to the back of the room, on the left side. Does this make any sense to someone in that area?" I asked as I pointed to the rear of the auditorium.

"Yes!" a woman answered. Audrey stood up. Her mother came into focus right behind her. "That was my mother's favorite song from *Funny Girl*. It *must* be my mother."

The next thing that came into my mind astounded me. This ghost had a great sense of humor. She was patting her rear end and smiling. "She is giving me the sense of her 'fanny.'"

The audience burst into laughter.

"Yes! That was her name," screeched Audrey. "Fanny . . . as in Fanny Brice. That is why she loved that song. Oh, wow!"

Then suddenly two other women stood up next to Audrey. They were Fanny's two other daughters, Audrey's sisters, and they had traveled quite a way to come to the event that day. It was obvious to me that Fanny was totally indifferent to these daughters because she communicated, *It's the least they could have done.*

I did not mention what Fanny said because some things are better left unsaid. Furthermore, I did not want to get into the middle of a family squabble.

Fanny then gave me an impression. "Your mother is talking about an operation for her leg."

Suddenly the other daughter, Meryl, spoke up. "Yes, that's right. She went into the hospital for an angioplasty."

Fanny blurted out, "Yes, but that is not what killed me. My heart stopped."

All three girls bent their heads.

Fanny began to send me visions and thoughts of her passing. Luckily, there was a chair onstage. I had to sit down because the message was so detailed.

"She is showing me that she woke up to see her mother, father, and sister standing next to her. She was in a bed. The room looked very much like a room that she had when she was younger."

I immediately got an impression that there was a window that overlooked a lake. I asked Meryl, "Do you know of such a place?"

"Yes. I know. Our grandparents owned a summerhouse near Castle Rock Lake. They used to bring the whole family there."

I continued describing the information that Fanny impressed on me.

"Your grandparents told your mother to rest a little, and she fell into a light slumber. The next thing she knew, she was standing in a field of sunflowers."

"Sunflowers were her favorite," said Audrey.

"She shows me that many people came to greet her. Some of them were people she knew from Wisconsin. Does that make sense?"

"That's where she grew up," exclaimed Meryl.

"Did she see a light or anything?"

"No, not that she remembers," I replied. "She recalls the night before the angioplasty, and the family being in the hospital. The rest is a blur until she saw her parents."

"What is she going to do over there?" Audrey asked.

Fanny quickly answered. *Rest! I have looked after you three enough. Now it's my turn!*

The entire audience enjoyed the delightful communication, and all wished Fanny well on her journey.

From what I have been told by spirits, it seems very common that when they first pass and return to their spiritual home, they are brought to a place (usually the childhood home) that looks identical to the environment they had on earth. If it is a home, everything, right down to the furniture and aromas, will be the same as the spirit remembers it.

THE LADY IN THE CHURCH

Some souls wait around for that special someone to come for them and bring them into the light. Others return to the place where they died because it brings them much comfort. Some are confused and go through the same routine as if they were still alive, as you will see from the following.

I flew back to New York to attend my cousin's wedding. On my way into the church, I noticed an elderly lady kneeling in a pew on the left side of the last row. She seemed to be completely unaware that a wedding was about to take place.

I sat down in one of the front pews and looked back. The woman in the last row was gone. I wondered where she went, so I glanced around the church. The organ music started, and the procession began. During the ceremony, I would occasionally crane my neck around toward the back of the church to see if the old woman had come back. On one of these instances, I saw her sitting in the last row. However, I also saw a man walk right through her to sit down. That's when I realized that I had been seeing a ghost.

When the wedding was over and everyone was on the front steps taking pictures, I walked back inside the church to see if the ghost was still there. Indeed, she was. This time I noticed that she was wearing a black dress and black sweater and holding on to a pair of black rosary beads. When I knelt down next to her, she looked my way. I looked right at her and sent her a message that I could see her. She told me, *There is no speaking in church, young man.*

I realized that she did not know that she was dead. I asked her, *How long have you been here?*

She mentally whispered, *Come to seven o'clock Mass every morning. Haven't missed one yet. Afterwards, I stay and say the rosary.*

What's your name? I asked.

Shh ... Hilda. She was quiet for a few minutes before saying, *Father Pat doesn't look good. I think he might be sick.*

Hilda continued to say her prayers, and I sat with her for a while. Then she disappeared, and I got up and walked out.

At the reception, I mentioned my ghostly encounter to one of my relatives. Soon the word got around, and everyone asked me questions about the ghost in church.

An elderly gentleman came over and introduced himself. "My name is Ed. I used to be an usher at the church. When someone told me what you saw, I thought I might talk to you about it. Everyone knew about Hilda. She came to church every morning dressed in black."

"Do you know when she died?" I asked.

"She died in March 1970, a week after Father Pat died. She had a heart attack right there in the pew."

I wondered why she acted as if she were still alive. I was sure that by then Father Pat would have escorted her into the spirit world.

Months after the wedding took place, my cousin sent me photos. Someone had taken a picture of me kneeling in the back of the church. Next to me was a bright, round orb of light. It had to be Hilda.

I believe that Hilda loved her daily early morning Mass so much that she stayed confined to the earth realm because of it. When a soul like Hilda is tied so strongly to earth through beliefs and habits, it can take a while to move into the heavenly realms. Through prayer and other means, the living can help those between dimensions to move on. That was my hope for Hilda.

DEATH BY SUICIDE

Sometimes I bring through messages from souls who took their own lives. It's always difficult to talk about suicide. When I wrote my first book, *Talking to Heaven*, I explained that people who commit suicide sometimes find themselves in a limbolike existence. Unfortunately, some readers thought I was referring to the state of "limbo" that is part of the Catholic belief system. That's not exactly what I meant.

When a person commits suicide, sometimes the soul feels a tremendous amount of guilt and anguish until it understands the effects of its suicide on loved ones. Because the ghost is in a highly distressed state of mind, it may stay in the same place where it last experienced life. For such a soul, such an existence can feel like self-induced torture. Rest assured, however, the majority of souls who die by their own hand are usually met by compassionate spiritual beings who help them to overcome their despair. Nonetheless, suicide has agonizing consequences for the whole family.

Forest Lawn Cemetery in the Hollywood Hills is close by Universal Studios, where *The Ghost Whisperer* is filmed. I had some time off one day, so I decided to pay my respects to a very good friend who had recently passed over and was buried at Forest Lawn. As I walked back to my car, I noticed a woman sitting at a grave site brushing away leaves on the gravestone. As I drew near her, she looked up at me, and our eyes met.

"Hello," I said to her. I pointed to the picture of the soldier on the headstone that was engraved with the words LOVING SON.

"Was he a tragedy of the war?" I asked.

"No," she replied. "A tragedy of life."

I knew that she needed some consoling, so I sat down and spoke with her. I didn't want to tell her what I did. I was there to listen to what she had to say.

"My name is Janice. This is my son Peter."

The following is the gist of what Janice told me about Peter.

Peter had everything he could want in life. He was an intelligent young man. His loving parents, Janice and Mike, and devoted siblings, Jake and Susan, doted on him. They all thought the world of him. Peter had been an honor student and a leader, and he had just entered his senior year of high school. Apparently, that is when everything changed for the worse. Some of Peter's schoolmates introduced him to a girl named Stacey, and the two of them became very close. Unfortunately, Stacey was not the wholesome type, and Janice and Mike didn't like Peter going out with her. "We thought she was a very bad influence on him," Janice candidly remarked.

Soon Peter's grades dropped, and he often missed classes and sometimes a day or two of school at a time. Janice and Mike noticed that Peter's old friends no longer came by. "When he began staying out later and later, we had our suspicions. Then again, we thought he might just be going through a phase," Janice continued. However, Janice's suspicions were confirmed when her daughter, Susan, found a hypodermic needle in Peter's laundry bag. Jake and Susan had also noticed a change in their big brother's behavior. The person they could always count on was never around anymore to help with homework or to take them to the movies.

Janice tried a variety of things to help her son. She attempted to homeschool him, but Peter resented it. "You've made me the way I am," Peter told her. "I'm not the perfect son you want." Janice said that his words stabbed her in her heart. "I never had any sort of expectation of Peter. I was merely a proud mother."

After Peter barely graduated from high school, Janice learned about tough love and wanted so much for her son to straighten out. "I had a brother in Minnesota who had a farm, and he agreed to take in Peter and Jake and have them work the farm for the summer." Janice gave Peter an ultimatum. "I told him that it was either the job or the street." She and Mike had to make the decision not to put up with Peter's disrespectful behavior anymore. At that point, Peter realized that he had no alternative. He resented his parents, but went to the farm anyway. After the first month, the old Peter seemed to have come back to life. He was happy and playful and back to his old self. Janice thought that Peter had turned a corner, but she was wrong. Her brother called to tell her that Peter had left the farm and he had no idea where the young man had gone.

Not knowing what to do, Janice called the police and listed Peter as a missing person. A month later, Peter was found living with Stacey in a tenement on the edge of town. By then, he was a full-fledged junkie. Once again, Peter blamed his mother. "It's all your fault. You were never happy with me as me."

Janice and Mike had made many attempts to get Peter clean and sober, but after several stints in drug rehab Peter had returned to his heroin addiction. Janice had to face the fact that the addiction had a strong grip on her son, and there was very little that she could do except pray. Janice's faith was strong, but it seemed that only a miracle would help.

Then something interesting happened. Peter broke off with Stacey and returned home. He said he didn't want to hurt his family anymore and wanted to grow up. By then, Peter had joined the Marines. "He said that he wanted to become a man. His father and I were very proud of Peter's decision."

After Peter sailed through basic training, he was immediately sent to the war in Iraq. He was a good soldier who felt he had something to prove, not only to himself but also to his family. "We all worried about Peter, but at least we knew where he was and what he was doing." Peter finished three tours of duty in Iraq before being honorably discharged. The whole family was so sure that Peter had become a changed man. To them, he was certainly a hero in every respect.

However, within a year after his discharge, Peter was back on heroin. On Christmas morning 2004, Janice and Mike found their son dead in his room from a drug overdose.

After Janice finished her story, I told her that I was very sorry for her tragic loss. I could feel her hurt and pain. At that moment, I heard the sound of whimpering behind me. It was very distinct, so I looked around. There sat a young man.

I'm Peter, he told me. I could tell he was also in a lot of pain. He said he hadn't slept in a long time and felt like he was in a nightmare. I asked him to look around and tell me what he saw.

It's very dark here, and people are crying. He then described what happened at death. *I woke up, but I could not get back into my body. I could hear my mother crying.*

I mentally sent Peter the thought that he was free now.

I feel imprisoned by my own thoughts, and it's hell. I feel so guilty for blaming my mother for my own problems. Now I see very clearly how much I hurt her. All I want to do is tell her I'm sorry.

At this point, I had to explain to Janice about my abilities. She wept. "I've been sitting here asking for a sign that my son was all right."

"Your son is in a lot of pain because of the guilt he feels," I said to Janice. "Many came to get him and bring him through the tunnel of light, but he refused to go. Do you understand?"

Janice wiped the tears from her eyes.

"Your son feels that he doesn't deserve happiness. He can't leave until you know how sorry he is for not loving you in the way you deserved. He says that he blamed you for his life turning out the way it did because he didn't want to take responsibility for it."

Janice relayed a story about Peter when he was nine years old. "There was this sudden rainstorm, and I was outside trying to finish up my gardening. Peter yelled from the porch to come inside before I got sick, but I stayed out another half hour to finish. Naturally, the next morning I was sick with a fever and cold. Peter took care of me. He made me breakfast and stayed by my side like a good little nurse. He even read to me. He was a great son who loved me very much."

As Janice told her story, I could see Peter's arms wrap around his mother in a hug. She could feel his energy around her. She looked up to the heavens and said, "I love you, Peter. You are my son, and I forgive you! I just want you to be happy!"

With those words, Peter's energy changed. He seemed mentally and emotionally lighter. His features became clearer and sharper to me. He thanked me and gave his mother a final message.

"He wants you to know that be it rain or shine, he will always love you."

Peter was finally free to go, and in an instant he was gone. Janice too was free. She could miss her son and mourn his loss, but she could go on living her life, knowing that she would see Peter again on the other side.

Like Peter, there are many spirits who are confused and distressed because of unfinished earthly business. Fortunately, Peter was able to communicate his feelings through me to his mother, make amends, and move on. However, some spirits are not so fortunate. Even if spirits know they are dead, they may be afraid to leave their familiar surroundings, or, like Hilda, they continue to live their memory patterns over and over again, stuck in their earthly mind-sets. They are literally bogged down by material concerns and earthly comforts and trapped between the earth and spirit worlds. They become what are known as earthbound spirits.

FOUR

The Undead

As mentioned, when a ghost decides to stay close to the earth plane for whatever reason, it literally becomes earthbound. There are a variety of reasons why a ghost remains tied to earth.

- A person has some sort of unfinished business with someone on earth.

- Death was sudden and unexpected, such as a car accident or murder, and the deceased is unaware of his or her condition.

- A person may want to make sure that his or her final wishes are being followed.

- A person with certain religious beliefs may be afraid of what lies ahead, especially if those beliefs tie into hell and damnation.

Because earthbound spirits reside in a very vivid mental and emotional state, their feelings and thoughts are extremely powerful.

An earthbound spirit can be relentless in its desire to get what it wants. Imagine a situation in your life that you thought about over and over until it became an obsession. Perhaps you stubbornly stuck to a particular point of view and would not budge. An earthbound spirit can have the same obsessive nature, only magnified one-hundredfold. Once a soul realizes its mistakes and burns out the desire to follow obsessive behavioral patterns, it can move on.

Many a ghost has stayed behind because of unfinished family business. Perhaps a husband died without telling his wife where he left the insurance policy, and without it she could be destitute. The husband will attempt to get through to her in any way possible, no matter how long it takes, to let her know about the policy. He will stay until the situation is resolved.

UNDER THE INFLUENCE

Contrary to the typical ghost story, earthbound ghosts do not aimlessly wander around deserted landfills and cemeteries. On the contrary, they are extremely attracted to the energy of the living and move about in areas where life is flourishing. They use the living's life force to sustain their power. These ghosts are very influential and can sometimes cause the living to engage in activities that they might not normally do.

My friend Laura recently told me about her experience with earthbounds. It was 1995, and she had just moved into a little house in an area of Los Angeles called Venice. In the sixties, Venice was overrun with drug dealers, hippies, and Hell's Angels. There were many violent crimes and drug-related deaths in that area at that time.

"The moment we moved in, I felt very upset," Laura said. "I didn't want to stay in the house at all and would find all sorts of excuses to leave. When I was out, I would want to stop in a grocery store for cigarettes, and you know, I don't smoke. But I had this overwhelming urge to buy cigarettes."

"What happened?" I asked.

"Well, I didn't buy the cigarettes. After a few months, I figured a ghost was haunting the house. I went to a psychic, and she said that there were two people living in the house and that they were huddled together on the floor of the small bedroom and didn't want to leave. She said they died in that very spot from an overdose of drugs."

"Oh, my God," I replied.

"She told me that the ghosts were the ones always sending me out for cigarettes."

"So what did you do?"

"The psychic and I concentrated our thoughts to get them to leave. It took hours before they would go, but they finally left. After that, I never felt the urge to leave the house and buy cigarettes again."

THE SAILOR

Another way a person becomes earthbound is by a traumatic death, like murder, or by an unexpected one, like a plane crash. In this type of scenario, the person may not realize he or she is dead for quite some time. In this postdeath state, a ghost may be living the illusion that he or she is still alive. I was once at a séance with Leslie Flynt, a very famous British medium. Leslie, the most tested medium of the twentieth century, was hailed as the number-one *physical* medium in the world. A physical medium is rare and very different from a mental medium. Mental mediums utilize their mental processes, such as seeing, hearing, and feeling, to contact spirits. Physical mediums contact spirits through their own physical bodies. A ghost uses the medium's physical energy and forms into a shape that becomes physically visible, or it uses the medium's voice to speak. The latter method was how ghosts came through Leslie Flynt.

As a group of us sat in a circle, the ghost of a young British sailor from World War II came through. He reported that he was part of a naval blockade attempting to intercept German U-boats. He added that his ship had been hit, and he was in the sea holding on to a rock. The poor soul was confused about his circumstances. He thought that if he let go of the rock he would drown. His mental image was so strong that he dared not let go.

The compassionate light created by the séance had attracted this particular soul to us. In fact, the people in the group were part of a rescue circle, and they did this sort of thing on a regular basis. Leslie impressed upon this young man that he was already dead. At first, the sailor found it hard to believe. As other members of the group instructed him to think of his deceased mother, the sailor's mother showed up to assist him into the light. When the young man realized the truth, he was ready to move on. You may be wondering why his mother, or some other deceased family member, had not come to him earlier and helped him out. The answer is simple. The young man was so obsessed by his situation that, with his whole heart and soul, he believed he was holding on to that rock. As long as he did, he felt he would not die. He was in such a highly charged emotional state that he couldn't imagine anything outside of his own predicament. Even if his mother had sat beside him, he would not have seen her.

Earthbound ghosts are often lost souls, and they need help to move out of the earthly realm and into the higher light. Sometimes they need the help of the living to cross over. This is where sensitivity and awareness come in. There are many of us who can help these lost souls move on.

Several years ago, I was host of my own syndicated television show, *Beyond*. We decided to produce a segment on paranormal activity, so we went on location to Oklahoma City to film a haunted house. It was the middle of summer, and I can remember how very hot it was. When we arrived at our hotel, I was greeted by Mary Ann Winkowski, a real-life ghost-buster who was going to be with me on the show. I will never forget my first impression of her. She seemed like a typical suburban housewife who would be more at home baking cookies than chasing ghosts. She had an especially good sense of humor and a wonderful way of making fun of herself and the work she did for a living. Needless to say, Mary Ann and I hit it off right from the start.

That night, Mary Ann, the production staff, and I had dinner together. As we waited for our meal to be served, Mary Ann described her life in detail. "The first time I realized that I was different was when I was about five years old. My grandmother caught me talking to my dead grandfather. 'You have the gift,' she said."

Mary Ann continued. "I often communicated with spirit children in my backyard. When my friends came over to play, they would ask, 'Who are you talking to?' It wasn't easy to say back then, 'I see dead people.'"

"When did you know you were a medium?" I asked.

Mary Ann quickly corrected me. "I am not a medium, James. I don't communicate with spirits that have passed to the other side. The only ones I see and hear are those who are earthbound."

Mary Ann explained her take on earthbound ghosts.

"When an earthbound wants to hang around and cause problems for the living, I usually get a call," she said. "Ghosts tell me their birthdays, death dates, the names of the cemeteries they're buried in, names of family members, what kind of jobs they had, and so on. I ask them to tell me what's troubling them. They usually tell me why they are hanging around and what they want. I feel it's my job to help earthbounds move on, so after the ghost tells me what's on its mind, I imagine a white light on the wall and ask the ghost to go into the light. Sometimes they do, sometimes they don't."

Then she said something that caught the staff by surprise.

"Ghosts prefer places that are crowded with people. They like to feed off the living's energy. They need the energy to give them the power to remain earthbound."

There was a gasp, then dead silence.

One of the production assistants was brave enough to ask, "Are there any ghosts here now?"

Suddenly Mary Ann's face froze as her eyes darted around the room. "Yes. I can see three of them. Two men and a woman. The man and woman came to the restaurant attached to someone in the far corner, and the other man comes here all the time because it's his favorite spot. He enjoys the smell of charbroiled meat."

Sensing that everyone wanted to hear more, Mary Ann continued. "Ghosts almost always attach themselves to friends and relatives. It's not unusual for them to follow their loved ones around."

That evening Mary Ann entertained us all with her ghostly tales, and especially stories about her work with the FBI and local police agencies.

"One night, as I was sleeping, I heard a noise," said Mary Ann. "I awakened to see my friend Thomas standing at the foot of my bed." She explained that Thomas was a DEA (Drug Enforcement Administration) agent; the two of them had worked together many times on murder cases.

Mary Ann continued. "I asked Thomas, 'What are you doing in my bedroom?' He answered, 'I was just killed, and you're the only one who can tell my partner who killed me and where to find my body.'"

Mary Ann explained that Thomas had gone undercover to investigate a drug ring and one of the dealers found out his true identity. Thomas was killed, and his body dumped in a swamp south of Cleveland. When Mary Ann conveyed this information to the police, Thomas's body was recovered, and eventually his killer was captured.

After dinner, we were too wound up to sleep, so we decided to take a drive to the location site. Mary Ann and I were anxious to determine if there were indeed any ghosts haunting the house. As we drove up the street, I glanced over at Mary Ann. She had a strange, trancelike look on her face and was very quiet. I decided to close my eyes. Jeff, our producer, drove the car at a snail's pace while looking for the house number. Suddenly Mary Ann and I shouted in unison, "Stop!" Jeff slammed on the brake, and the car screeched to a halt in front of a brown-shuttered, clapboard house.

"Can you see the dark energy over the rooftop?" I asked.

"Yeah . . . looks like a dome of clouds," Mary Ann replied.

By the size of the shadowy mass surrounding the house, we figured there were a number of ghosts haunting it. I squeezed Mary Ann's hand. At last I had found a long-lost, kindred spirit.

The next morning we arrived at the haunted house raring to go. The owners waited at the side door to welcome us. Beth, the wife, seemed a little too happy to have ghosts living in her home. I whispered to Mary Ann, "Do you think she'll give us trouble?" Mary Ann nodded. "She may not want them to go."

Mary Ann suddenly began to turn her head in all different directions. "There's an older man here. His name is William. He was born in 1857 and died in 1935. He is here to protect the young boy." I followed Mary Ann into a bedroom. We could tell it was the owner's young son's room by the toys and games scattered around.

As we entered the room, Mary Ann uttered, "There is a little boy named Jimmy at the end of the bed."

"Ask him why he feels the need to be here," I said.

"Because he never had the toys this boy has," she responded. "He is fascinated by all these electronic gadgets and often plays alongside the other boy. He also has a speech impediment. He's afraid of being alone. The old man was buried right next to the little boy, so he stays with the boy to keep him company. The little boy says he is not ready to leave."

"Where are they buried?"

"Holy Cross Cemetery, not far from here."

Mary Ann added, "There are two other ghosts that visit this house, but they don't stay for long periods of time. One is a nineteen-year-old boy named Harold Spratt. He died in a car accident. He follows the teenage girl who lives in this home and comes around every now and then. He says he likes her energy and finds her attractive."

"Are you telling me this ghost is a pervert?" I blurted out.

"He's a typical nineteen-year-old. In his ghostly body, he can do things and be places he never could before."

"He's a Peeping Tom, then!" I said. The thought of this ghost following around the teenage girl grossed me out.

"The other ghost is Johnson. He was sort of the neighborhood busybody. He had a heart attack and died in his garage. He especially doesn't like the people who bought his house next door, so he hangs around just to cause trouble."

I asked the owners about the next-door neighbor. They verified that they did have a neighbor named Mr. Johnson who died of a heart attack in the garage.

"He was always complaining about something," said Beth. When we told Beth that he was still hanging around, she almost jumped in the air. "I bet he's the one causing all the problems for that young couple. They're always having some kind of trouble with the plumbing and electricity."

Mary Ann warned the daughter to always protect herself by visualizing a white light around her. "That goes for all of you," she continued. "You don't want to bring any wayward ghosts into your home anymore."

Mary Ann asked the owners, "Do you want me to create a portal of light so the ghosts can cross over? Once I do, and if they go into the light, you will definitely notice a change in the atmosphere of the house. It will feel more peaceful."

Beth replied, "I hate to see them go. It's already making me sad because I know I will miss them. Are you sure there isn't any other way that they can stay and not bother us?"

Mary Ann and I looked at each other, thinking, *Uh-oh.*

"If you keep them here, it really wouldn't be fair to them," I explained. "They're spirits, and they need to continue on their journey. The best thing to do is to set them free from the shackles of this earth plane."

Beth was stubborn. The ghosts not only made her feel special but were fodder for good gossip. It's ironic that we, the living, can just as easily keep the dead around with our thoughts as the dead can manipulate us with theirs.

Finally Beth gave in, and Mary Ann began to concentrate. "I am creating a white light on the wall, sort of like a doorway." The moment she began her visualization, everyone in the room, including the crew, felt an immediate difference in the atmosphere, as if a weight had been lifted. The hairs on my arms stood up. I knew the ghosts were gone.

After lunch break, Jeff came over to me. "I need more footage. Having Mary Ann create a light in her mind is great, but it doesn't do a lot for our television audience."

"Maybe we should try to find the cemetery she mentioned and locate the graves of these ghosts," I suggested.

Jeff asked the owner for the yellow pages and jotted down the cemetery's address. We all jumped into the cars and drove about twenty minutes to Holy Cross Cemetery. I was so excited at the thought of finding the ghosts' graves. I thought to myself, *James, only you could get this excited about going to a cemetery.*

Although the cemetery was only average in size, it took us a while to locate the graves, and the unbearable heat was taking its toll. Maybe my bright idea wasn't so bright after all. We seemed to be going around in circles, searching for the graves of the young boy and the old man. My brain was fried. Pretty soon we wouldn't have to look any further, I figured, since I would have died from heat stroke and the show would be canceled.

"Guys, I have to take a break," I called out. I sat under a shade tree with a bottle of water to cool off. The crew kept hunting. I just closed my eyes and wondered how much longer it would take to find the graves—if we ever found them.

Suddenly I felt a tugging at my pant leg. I opened my eyes and saw a little boy dressed in knickers, a vest, a jacket, and a hat. He opened his mouth and spoke with a whistling sound. *I'm Zimmy . . . Zimmy McKevit. My body is over there.* He pointed to the second row of graves on my right. I stood up in shock and turned in the direction of the grave site, and then back again. In that split second, the little boy had disappeared. I walked over to the row of graves, and sure enough, there it was. Next to Jimmy's headstone was the headstone of William Arling, born 1857, died 1935. I felt excitement run through me like a boy opening gifts on Christmas morning.

I called out to the crew, "Hey, guys, I think I found something."

No longer bound to the earth, the two ghosts were free to move on, but I am sure that they still hang around the familiar surroundings, not to haunt but perhaps to protect.

I knew that Mary Ann and I were kindred spirits. We had done this work before in other lives, and we were together again in this life to help people understand the world of ghosts. Mary Ann was someone special, and I wanted to share her gift with the rest of the world. Eventually, *The Ghost Whisperer* became a TV show based on her life's work.

A GHOST'S OBSESSION

One doesn't automatically change his or her mental and emotional mind-set after death. If one is obsessed with money, for instance, the worship of money is still there even after death. As the saying goes, "you can't take it with you"—but some try to. Ghosts obsessed with the money they left behind will try to control the purse strings from the other side by influencing their heirs with thoughts. This can be a tough lesson for people who just can't let go.

Annette Baker was a person who couldn't let go. She was once one of the most successful entertainment executives and producers in television. She fit the stereotype of an executive clawing her way to the top and stepping over the bodies along the way. When she was alive, she was a tyrant, barking orders and belittling others, to make sure everyone knew that she was in charge. Power was her "god."

During a meeting with the writers of *The Ghost Whisperer*, ghostly Annette appeared. She entered the office and immediately began looking over everyone's shoulder to see what was being written.

Then she spewed out a tirade of criticism. *What do they know? I produced some of the best shows on TV.*

Annette fussed around, saying how great she was and how no one had ever appreciated her. It was a blessing that none of the writers were aware of what was happening. After she finished praising herself, she made a hasty retreat into the hall, no doubt headed for the president of the studio to tell him a thing or two on how to run the place.

It is quite amazing how incredibly tied we are to our mental and emotional states. Guilt, anger, and resentment keep souls in self-imposed prisons even after they die. To move on, we must learn to forgive others as well as ourselves.

FRANKLY, MISS SCARLET . . .

Some ghosts have a difficult time letting go of their earthly lives because of fond memories of good times, unrequited loves, unrealized goals, and so forth. These earthbounds get so wrapped up in memories that they cannot let go of their past lives.

I sat in the lobby of the old David O. Selznick Studios in Culver City with my development executive, Danielle Butler, waiting for a three o'clock meeting with television producers to discuss possible shows for the next television season. David O. Selznick made some of the most extravagant and popular movies of the twentieth century. The offices were actually housed in the authentic plantation set seen in *Gone with the Wind*. The building had not been changed since. Suddenly the hairs on my arm stood on end. I sensed a lot of ghostly activity in the lobby, especially around the long, winding staircase. I had been in many studios in L.A., communicating with deceased television and movie personalities who had been hanging around their old environs for years, but this was the first time I had encountered so many ghosts in one place.

As I looked up the staircase, I could see the balustrade that surrounded the various offices on the second floor. A multitude of ghosts dressed in various costumes milled around these offices. A group of ghosts wearing khaki uniforms walked up the stairs. They looked as if they came right out of a war movie made in the early 1950s. At the same time, several chorus girls with colorful outfits passed them on their way down.

I turned and whispered to Danielle, "This place is definitely haunted." Just then, I looked up and was immediately drawn to a woman descending the staircase wearing a yellow plantation dress and a yellow bow wrapped around her hair. She bowed her head and continued moving. A black gentleman who tapped down the steps followed her. I recognized the legendary Bill "Bojangles" Robinson from the Shirley Temple movie *The Littlest Rebel*.

It was quite an amazing experience of ghostly activity. When I went into my meeting, the first thing out of my mouth was, "Do you know how haunted this place is?" The producers just stared at me, completely unaware that they shared their environment with ghosts from another era.

Time spent on earth is one of learning. From a spiritual point of view, all that is expected of us is to love ourselves—not in a narcissistic sense, but to value ourselves for the spiritual beings we are. We are here to do the best we can and to treat others with compassion and kindness. The human level is a great school where our souls can learn and grow. If we can understand this, our transition to the other side can be easy and joyful.

Eventually, earthbound ghosts live out all of their earthly desires and have a sense that they want to experience something more. When they do, they are ready to move into the higher mental and spiritual dimensions.

FIVE

The Spirit World

Over and over, I have been asked, "Where is the spirit world?" Unfortunately, there is no easy or simple answer to this question. To understand where and what the spirit world is, we must change our thinking. The spirit world is not a geographic place per se, not a location that can be found on a map. The spirit world is truly a state of energetic *being*.

The universe is made up of electromagnetic waves. We may not be physically aware of these waves of energy, but we know they exist because we see images on our televisions, we hear voices on our cell phones, and we eat food that is cooked in microwave ovens. These waves are individually and precisely tuned to a particular frequency so that they can function properly.

Like the electromagnetic waves of our physical universe, the spirit world consists of thousands, perhaps millions, of energy dimensions, and each one has its own distinct vibration. These vibrations overlap one another and therefore penetrate our physical world. Like the Internet, the spirit dimensions can interact with people all around the world without one person ever having to leave the privacy of his or her home. We may be unaware of the

multitude of vibrations that surround us, but they exist nevertheless. Unfortunately, most people cannot tune in to these vibrations without some sort of training.

The dimensions of the spirit world are akin to the message in
the Bible in John 14:2: "In my Father's house are many mansions:
if it were not so, I would have told you." I believe the "mansions"
referred to here are the various spiritual dimensions. As a
medium, I have the ability to penetrate these dimensions by rais-
ing my vibration to higher frequencies. Thus, I am able to be a
conduit between the lower, slower physical world and the faster,
vibratory dimensions of the unseen spiritual world. We can all be
conduits if we put time and effort into it. One of the fastest ways
to heighten our vibrations is through meditation.

SPIRITUAL DIMENSIONS

Many years back, I was honored to meet Mark Macy, a dedicated
research scientist who, like me, was interested in providing detailed proof of life after death. Much of his work has been overlooked and remains so to this day. Macy was at the forefront of
investigations into the various means by which ghosts communicate with the living. He was involved with World Instrumental
Trans-Communication, an organization of researchers who used
various technologies such as radio, television, and computers to
bring forth messages and communication from the spiritual
world. I have studied Macy's work for years and find that much
of the information he has collected closely resembles the ghostly
descriptions I have received through my own psychic work.

As I explain the various levels of the spirit world, please remember that I do so based on my own spiritual evolvement. A ghost
who wants to express the color red through me is limited by what I

understand as the color red. The ghost has to use my frame of reference. Another medium might have a different interpretation of the color red based on his or her frame of reference. Also, the dimensions of the spirit world are not easy to describe. I am limited by inadequate human terms. It is often difficult to describe dimensions that are ethereal and celestial. I find it frustrating when I try to explain the incredible visions, colors, and feelings that are being communicated to me. Words don't do the spiritual realms justice.

When we leave our physical bodies in death, we enter a very finely tuned dimension. As discussed in the last chapter, everyone's experience upon entering the spirit world is different depending on their belief system, their level of fear or ignorance, and their spiritual evolvement. As we pass through the lower astral level and move to the higher dimensions of the astral world, the experiences become even more rarefied. Thoughts and feelings are heightened in intensity. Ghosts travel to various dimensions until they reach a dimension that coincides with their level of awareness.

On earth many of us share lives with others who have completely different ideologies from our own. If we look around the world, we can see a multitude of religious beliefs and various ideas about how life works. We live with diversity because earth is our school, and we are here to learn from the differences everyone has to offer us. However, in the spiritual dimensions we gravitate to a dimension of like-mindedness and toward others who have the same points of view and are at the same level of evolvement as our own. We create with our thoughts, words, and deeds, and how we have lived our lives is where we will end up after we die. If we follow a certain faith or religion, for example, we will be with others who share that same philosophy.

OUR FAITH MAKES IT SO

A few years ago, I did a reading with Malcolm Jamal Warner from *The Cosby Show*. Malcolm was and is a wonderful, creative, loving guy. In the middle of his reading, a very big woman who had died in a car accident showed up. She wore a yellow dress and a wide-brimmed white hat. She looked as if she were going to a Sunday church service.

She stood in front of me and said, *My name's Virginia, and I think you are doing the devil's work speaking with spirits.*

I asked her, *If I am evil, why did you show up?*

Because I love him.

That is why I do this work . . . out of love.

She was insistent. *No, the devil is putting words in your mouth.*

Are you the devil? I asked.

She was flabbergasted. *Of course not.*

Eventually, she began to understand what I was getting at. However, she continued to relay various biblical passages to me.

As I transmitted the messages to Malcolm, he smiled. "That's my Auntie Virginia!"

This reading demonstrated how tenaciously we can hold on to our die-hard beliefs. How do we change such beliefs? We have to be open to change. When we are able to see love and healing and think of people as good, not evil, we may be able to change our perspective on life in general. It helps to question our beliefs. Our thoughts are powerful. Loving thoughts open our hearts. Loving thoughts help those in the lower spiritual dimensions find the truth.

THE LOWER ASTRAL PLANE

When a person sheds his or her physical body at the time of death, the silver cord that once tethered the etheric body to the physical body is severed. What remains is an exact replica of the physical body, only one that is lighter, subtler, and more vibrant.

The very first dimension beyond the physical realm that a ghost encounters is the lower astral dimension, which vibrates very close to the earth's realm and is located between the earth and the higher spheres. Many ghosts have communicated that this level is gray and dim and reminds them of the foggy mists of San Francisco Bay. Ghosts usually do not linger in this lower astral level very long. Only the unevolved remain in this dark world.

On the lower astral level, thoughts are heard and seen very clearly. Ghosts cannot hide their thoughts as humans can. In fact, the mentally charged lower astral world amplifies all thoughts and emotions. I often refer to this world as our mental and emotional garbage dump. When ghosts decide to stay in this lower astral dimension, they become a collective creation of aspects of humans that are obsessively tied to unresolved emotions, usually negative in nature, such as anger, depression, desperation, loneliness, guilt, addiction, cruelty, and hatred. The lower astral world is bleak because ghosts seem to feed off the negativity associated with this collective creation. It's as if ghosts are bound by a very strong mind-hold. Because thoughts remain with us on our journey, our points of view also stay with us. Beliefs, likes, dislikes, and judgments remain exactly the way they were. There are no instant, all-knowing miracles or revelations when we die.

I am often asked, "What if a person doesn't believe in an afterlife?" A person who doesn't believe there is life after death will be quite surprised to find that they are still alive. It may take a long time for them to realize what has happened, and during that time they will roam the lower astral realm. Thought controls existence, and so whatever one believes is what one gets.

THE SCREAMS

The lower astral level contains many fragmented, nonhuman, unevolved astral bodies and thought forms created by fear. All thoughts are alive here. Judgments, prejudice, spiritual ignorance, and misunderstandings make up these fragmented thought forms. These thoughts linger in this realm as pockets of dark energy. Many Christians refer to the lower astral level as hell. It is not fire and brimstone, as we are told, but remnants of negative thoughts.

After I decided to devote time to my psychic development, one of the first places I experienced in my exercises was the lower astral realm. I usually tell this anecdote in my workshops, and afterward people come over and share very similar experiences with me.

I had just awakened one Sunday morning and was still in a twilight state, somewhere between the dream and waking states. I remember the feeling of floating down into my body from a very high spiritual place, as if I were falling off a cliff. The sensation was not scary, but more like going down a fast-moving elevator. I can recall it very distinctly because I kept going down into what seemed to be a crevice in the earth, and it became darker and darker until it was almost pitch-black. It was eerie and upsetting. I heard people screaming. I saw and felt arms reaching out of the darkness trying to grab a hold of me. They were not fully formed bodies, so I surmised them to be thought forms and fragmented energies that saw my light and wanted to clutch on to it. I knew these fragmented energies could not hurt me, but still, I felt very uncomfortable. When I opened my eyes, I thought, *Oh, my God, that was a scary, dark place.* I believe that I was being shown this particular level so that I would know it existed. It was important to be aware of all the places on the other side, and it was also important that I teach others about the existence of these places.

During one of my TV demonstrations, I witnessed something I had not seen before. While tuning in to a young woman in the audience, I immediately became aware of an older, unkempt female spirit pulling the strands of her hair as if it were made of string. This ghost stood to the participant's right side, and I knew immediately that it was her mother. I was a little scared to proceed because of what I saw and felt. Around the mother was a dark brown, tarlike energy that I could only describe as "dirty energy." I knew instinctively that this ghost was on a very low level of the astral world.

The mother faced her daughter and was screaming profanities at her. Each time the mother articulated her negative energy toward her daughter, I noticed the daughter would bow her head lower. This was my cue to protect myself, so I quickly pictured a wall of golden light between the ghost and me. It was a wall of protection to keep this lower astral entity's negative energy away from me. (This is a quick technique for instant protection against harmful and depressing energy.)

I told the young woman, "Your mother is very angry and is blaming you for all of the bad luck she had in life."

The woman's head just bowed even lower.

I felt sorry for this woman because I could tell that she was very sweet and had a beautiful spirit. However, the years of mental torture and abuse by her mother had stolen her youthful innocence.

I got the sense that the mother was a drunk and had had a heroin addiction during her earthly life and that she never took responsibility for any of the wrong choices she had made. Instead, she blamed others for her predicament, became bitter from an unfulfilled life, and died penniless.

As a spirit, this woman entered the lower astral world, her same negative mind-set intact. Instead of attempting to break her old habits, she stayed in a perpetual misguided loop. This was all she knew, or all she wanted to know.

When I tried to help the ghost to understand her situation, she snapped back, *You don't know what you're talking about*. Then she mentioned that the other spirits who resided where she was were *nasty, angry people who never listen to me*. Interesting how like attracts like.

The ghost continued to yell at me. I turned to the young woman and said, "I'm going to ignore your mother because her behavior is atrocious." That made the ghost even angrier.

Nevertheless, I continued to counsel the young woman. "You know," I said, "you are not responsible for your mother's life."

The young woman looked at me and smiled, as if she had been waiting to hear those words her whole life but never had.

I ran into this young woman several years later. She told me that she had been in therapy and was a completely different person. She no longer kept her head bowed, but stood up straight, proud to be who she was.

"Are you still bothered by your mother?"

"I don't have dreams of her anymore. I now know she is in a place that she created by the way she lived her life. Whenever I think of her, I just send her love and blessings."

Not only is the lower astral realm made up of our collective negative thoughts and emotions, but we continually feed it through our negativity, including negative forms of entertainment. Violent movies, television shows, and music that exaggerate people's fears and cruel behavior may seem exciting, but they only exacerbate the baser thoughts of society. The creators of such negative images may be under the influence of ghosts of the lower astral world. All is energy, and negative energy like fear, anger, and hate becomes imbedded in the lower astral level. Like a vicious cycle, these thought forms come back to haunt us by causing more fear and hatred.

We talk a lot about saving the outside environment, but it all begins with the environment inside ourselves. I know it sounds clichéd and boring to think that love, peace, and kindness can save us, but it's true. Positive thoughts help to counterbalance negative energy. Our positive thoughts and prayers are vital to our physical and psychic well-being.

THE HIGHER ASTRAL DIMENSIONS

Just as there is a natural progression in life on earth, there is also a natural progression in the afterlife. As a ghost expands its awareness and develops its spiritual muscle, so to speak, it passes from one spiritual plane of existence to another. As it does, it becomes less attracted and less connected to earthly trappings.

Many spirits pass into the light of the higher astral dimensions and arrive in a place I refer to as Summerland. This dimension is almost as real as earth. It is a world of amazing buildings and homes, the colors of which are incomprehensible by earthly minds. Many spirits in these realms communicate that the houses in which they live look exactly like their houses on earth, except that they are perfect in every way. There are no plumbing or electrical problems, no water leaks or creaky staircases. They often describe each house sitting on a piece of property that is in perfect proportion to the size of the house. In other words, there is no such thing as urban sprawl. When we think of our perfect home here on earth, we are unconsciously creating its counterpart on the higher astral level. Spiritual assistants on the higher planes of the astral dimension help shape our homes by using our thoughts combined with their own mental power. By the time we arrive in heaven, our new home is waiting for us, perfectly attuned to our individuality and makeup.

In addition to homes, the higher dimensions include great buildings like music halls, museums, and libraries. Our thoughts are concrete on this level, so what we have been planning and thinking about actually materializes. All our dreams and desires can come true in the higher astral level. The greatest works of humankind are created first on the upper astral level. Many ghostly scientists work together in this realm focusing their energies so that new ideas filter down into human minds.

The higher astral dimension is also a place of divine inspiration; it is free of earthly needs and conflict. The spirits in these dimensions come together in love to expand their mental and spiritual horizons. It is a state of being where fine minds conceive incredible artistic creations. Anything that can make a heart sing is located here.

One last thing: spirits in the higher dimensions can visit others in the lower dimensions, but those in the lower dimensions cannot move to the higher dimensions until their souls are ready. Highly evolved spirits are very much aware of what happens on the physical levels and often visit family and friends on earth to aid and protect them.

THE PIANO MAN

I did a reading for a young lady named Pam whose father, Gus, had passed over. When Gus came through, he mentioned the name of Otto.

I asked Pam, "Does 'Otto' mean anything to you?"

"No, I don't remember hearing the name."

I continued, "I see a piano associated with Otto."

Pam could not think of any Otto in her father's life.

"When you go home, ask your mother if she knows anyone named Otto."

Pam's father kept on talking about the piano and taking lessons.

"I vaguely remember my father taking piano lessons maybe. I think he said he wasn't any good, so he stopped."

Pam paused. "I think there were many things in my father's life that he regretted not doing."

Gus sent me a thought. "Is there a tune you have in your head that you can't stop humming?"

Pam's eyes opened wide. "Yes! It is the most ridiculous thing. The last three weeks, whenever I'm in my car, the same tune pops into my head."

"He's saying, *It's me! I sang it to her when she was a baby.*"

Several weeks later, I received a letter from Pam. She had shared her reading with her mother. Her mother had heard about Otto from Pam's father. Otto was a Jewish piano teacher who was sent to Auschwitz when the Nazis invaded Poland. Gus was one of the first American troops to free the Jews from concentration camps in World War II, and that was where he met Otto. When Gus helped Otto out of the camp, Otto told him, "Music was the only thing that kept me alive."

Otto told Gus, "Music is the heart of the soul. It makes human beings remember where they come from."

Pam wrote that all the pieces of her father's message began to fit together. She knew that her father was with Otto and that Otto was teaching him the piano. The song she hummed was a song that her father had composed after he returned from the war.

LIFE GUIDES

Once ghosts leave the lower realms and travel into the higher spiritual planes, they meet a variety of other spirits of a higher nature. Mainly, these spirits act as guides to us on earth and are able to influence our thoughts and actions in positive ways. Some guides are connected to us throughout our soul's evolution; others are attracted to us because of the lessons we are here to learn. All guides are continuously evolving in their own right, and as part of their spiritual growth, they want to convey their knowledge and insight to many of us on earth. The following is a list of different types of spiritual guides.

Helper Guides

Helper guides influence and assist us by bringing out the innate talents imbedded within our soul's makeup. Usually, these guides had similar talents while on earth; their job now is to help the living utilize their abilities to the utmost and gain a clearer understanding of their talents, which can be anything from accounting to medicine to singing. In my workshops, I suggest that people call forth their helper guides when they are working on a project or just need help in their job. In Greek mythology, a helper guide is called a "muse"—a guide who assists us in reaching our dreams.

Relationship Guides

Relationship guides work with our unique energy vibration to open our hearts to love so that we can share our lives with another. They guide us in attracting persons with whom we are karmically connected. We may have lessons to learn with certain people, or there may be strong love bonds that have been carried over from other lifetimes. Also, we have many soul mates, not just one, and each soul mate is a part of our soul group. A soul mate bears gifts in the form of life lessons. Relationship guides always bring the right people to us at the right time. There are no mistakes. Every person in our lives is there for a reason. Every person we meet on earth is a potential teacher, even though we may not think so at the time, especially if those lessons are unpleasant and uncomfortable. Relationship guides also teach us to appreciate ourselves. When we feel worthy, we can understand the nature of true, unconditional love.

Family Guides

So often people come up to me and say, "I didn't choose my family." Oh, but yes, we do. Although this may be a challenge for some, we choose our family members before we enter the earth existence. In fact, our families have been with us through many lifetimes. It is interesting to know that souls travel collectively in groups. They often wait until they are all together on the other side so that when they decide to travel back to earth, they will arrive around the same time. Our families are a part of our soul group, and the experiences we share with our family members are probably the most difficult to understand and the most important to master.

I find that there is a lot of unfinished business among families because so much of the work that I do is communication with family members. The love bond between one member of a family and another can become even stronger after death. After they pass, many souls reach a realization that they could have been more cooperative, more understanding, or more helpful to their family. They sense that they could have been a better parent, husband, or child. It is very common for family members to decide to make up for their earthly mistakes by helping their families from the other side, becoming their spiritual guide.

A MOTHER'S LOVE

Many years ago, while I was honing my medium skills, I attended what I refer to as a "development circle," a group of like-minded people coming together to contact spirits. During one such circle, a colleague said, "Your mother is sitting next to you."

My mother and I were close when I was young. She under-stood my talent but didn't know how to explain it, especially to my father.

"She wants to let you know that she feels very guilty. She's sorry that she wasn't there for you when you were young. She was always afraid for you. She wants to be a true mother to you now."

I was both amazed and thrilled to hear these words. It was like having a mother's love all over again. From that moment on, I have always felt my mother's presence around me. She has been a guide to me ever since, encouraging me to love myself and nurturing me when I need someone to tell my troubles to. She is also excellent when it comes to warning me about certain situations and circumstances that may cause me harm. I have also learned to be more appreciative and compassionate with her by my side.

THE HEART OF A TEACHER

Ghosts that become guides to the living are indeed special. When spirits were unable to fulfill their desires to help someone while alive, or when they feel as though their work on earth was cut short, they will have opportunities on the other side to satisfy their desires and assist the living. That was the case with the two spirits in this next example of fulfilling one's life purpose not only on earth but in heaven as well.

I was doing a radio show in Los Angeles when a caller named Willie wanted to find out about his sister. I was not completely clear on what I was receiving, so I asked Willie if the vision I saw meant anything to him.

"I am seeing a beach and sunset."

"Yes, I understand that," replied Willie.

"Is your sister's name Mac, Mackie, something like that?"

"Maxine. We called her Max."

"She is here. She has a medium-size build and brown hair. Did she have highlights?"

"Yes."

"Her death came very quickly—it was a huge surprise to her. She is saying that she never expected this, that no one did."

I quickly became aware of being underneath water. "I feel that she's drowning—she could not get her footing. Do you understand this?"

Willie began to cry. "Yes, I understand."

"Now she is mentioning Amy. Do you know Amy?"

"Yes."

"She is with Amy now," I said.

"She went with Amy. They died together."

"I keep getting this feeling of being swept underwater."

Then I had some very weird visions. "I keep seeing things like trees and furniture flying by, and I am holding on to a doorway or what looks like a doorway. Your sister loses Amy. She says they couldn't hold on anymore. Is this correct?" I asked Willie.

Willie could barely hold it together. I knew that I had made a link between him and his sister, Maxine, and that this was their chance to reunite.

I continued. "I feel as though this is a terrible tragedy involving a lot of people."

"Yes, it was," he replies.

Then it hit me. "Was this the tsunami in Southeast Asia?"

"Yes," said Willie. "Max and Amy went there for Christmas vacation."

"Maxine wants me to tell you that she didn't experience anything painful except that she does remember debris hitting her. She wants Peter to know that she's okay."

"Peter is her husband," Willie added.

"She is telling me that she and Amy taught children together."

"Yes. They taught together in a preschool for ten years."

"Well, you know," I continued, "they were born teachers. There is nothing they loved better. Amy wants me to tell you that there won't be much rest for them over there."

Then Maxine said something I thought was very interesting. "Your sister is telling me that she is still teaching children on the other side. There are schools for different subjects. She is even mentioning that she is teaching the children who have passed over from the tsunami. She is telling me that race doesn't mean much in the other world. That it is only a misunderstanding of the earth world. Maxine is finding that one of the challenges over there is meeting spirits that still carry their prejudice and mind-sets from their old lives instead of opening themselves to the world before them. She says people have what they create. Maxine says that she and Amy forge ahead because they are dedicated to their students."

"Yes, I know that's what they're like," Willie responded. "Actually, both of them won awards from the county for their teaching." Willie paused. "Besides teaching, what else are they doing there?"

"Max says that they are involved with children who pass over to the spirit world and have no mother to guide them. In a way, they are foster mothers. They are helping kids who need their influence the most, and they work along with other family members. They are strong guides for the children's growth and evolution."

GUIDES OF A HIGHER ORDER

The following is a list of highly evolved spiritual guides whose tasks are to protect, inspire, and teach.

The Gatekeeper

This guide's main task is to protect us from any obtrusive energy (like earthbound ghosts) that might want to harm us. Gatekeepers make sure that only energies that are in sync with our soul's growth are brought through.

Inspirational Guide

This guide impresses us with spiritual teachings and truths such as compassion, forgiveness, and understanding. An inspirational guide helps us to see a situation from various points of view so that we can learn tolerance, kindness, and compassion, thus elevating our nature to higher awareness.

Healing Guide

As the name implies, this guide assists us with healing energies, helping to promote healing and well-being in our emotional, mental, and physical bodies. We do not need to ask for our guide's assistance because it knows when we need help.

Historical Guides

Uncanny as it may seem, there are many ghosts that get caught up in the emotionalism of a particular time period, and they want to stay in that vibration. You may have heard of the haunted battlefields of war. During the Civil War, more soldiers were killed in one day than during the entire Vietnam War. Those who died in battle during the Civil War identify deeply with that war and the ideals on each side. There is an incredible emotional charge associated with this particular period of history, and many a ghost still haunts the grounds on which he fought and clings to the beliefs for which he died.

Many ghosts also walk the halls of the White House and the chambers of Congress. I have encountered quite a few ghosts of former U.S. congressmen who regret that, having been given a rare opportunity to foster positive change in the country, they blew it. Many cling to the earth, guilt-ridden with failure, often haunting their assembly room in the hope of impressing their contemporaries.

In April 1996, I had a chance to visit two places in Washington, D.C., that I have always wanted to see. The first was the Capitol. The day I walked into that immense, ornate rotunda, I immediately felt its rich, impenetrable, swirling energy. Images and impressions of the past flooded my mind. As I rode the elevator to the second floor, I could sense the energy becoming thick and heavy. I entered the balcony of the Senate chamber and looked around at the empty space. The Senate was not in session that particular morning. I sat down and closed my eyes. Suddenly the smell of stale tobacco filled my senses, and I quickly peered over the railing to see rows and rows of desks no longer empty but humming with the sounds of men of the past. I could distinguish one group mingling together by their heavy black suits and hats, typical clothing from a century ago. Another group of men in gray flannel suits stood together smoking and laughing. It was eerie. I left the ghostly senators to their own devices and headed toward my second stop.

I was also anxious to see the Ford Theater, where President Lincoln was shot. Ever since I was a little boy, I have felt a particular connection to Abraham Lincoln. I could remember doodling at the family dining table when I was about eight and looking down at the drawing I had just made. It was of a Civil War soldier with blue eyes, a bushy mustache, and a blue cap on his head. It was not until I was in my twenties that I saw that picture again. I had pulled some things out of storage, and the drawing fell out of a book. This time when I looked at it, I gasped. It looked like the grown me, mustache and all. All that was missing was the blue military uniform. As I stared at the picture, I flashed on a memory of personally meeting Abraham Lincoln during his visit to a Civil War battlefield. That vision has stayed with me ever since.

Following that revelation, I remember a Sunday night several years back. I had trouble falling asleep and tossed and turned in bed trying to get comfortable. Out of the corner of my eye, I saw a figure at the end of my bed. I recognized the outline as Abraham Lincoln. He stood very tall and looked right through me. I noticed that other ghosts flanked him on either side, but I could not make out their identities.

I asked, *Are you Lincoln?*

He returned a thought. *That is the personality you know me by.*

The picture of the Civil War soldier popped into mind, and I just knew that I had been with Lincoln in another life.

Lincoln sent another thought. *I come with many others. We are the new order, and we have a message for you.*

I wanted to make sure that my mind wasn't playing tricks on me, so I asked once again, *Are you really Abraham Lincoln?*

His thoughts were piercingly clear to me. *We are of a new order and are here to assist you in your mission.*

This statement took me by surprise. *What mission?*

We are working with you to open the hearts and minds of everyone you touch and to bring a new awareness to many.

I still could not believe it was Lincoln talking to me. Being a stickler for details, I sent out another thought: *I need proof that it is really you.*

You shall have proof. You need only to remember what we came here to tell you.

Tomorrow is Monday, I said. *If I hear any reference made to Abraham Lincoln, I will know this conversation is for real.*

You will have your proof, but remember our words, Lincoln said as his figure disappeared from my sight.

I fell into a deep sleep, and the next thing I could hear was the ringing of my fax machine. I went downstairs to my office and watched the pages come through. They were from my book editor, Linda Tomchin. We had been working on the last part of my book *Heaven and Earth*. She was sending me her version of the last chapter, which consisted of questions and answers. This was the first time I had seen it. As I read over one of the questions, I was dumbstruck. "Are premonitions generally bad?" The answer she wrote was: "Premonitions usually forewarn of impending crisis or disaster. . . . Abraham Lincoln had a premonition after he was elected that . . ." I dropped the paper and sat down. Oh, my God," I exclaimed. Was this the proof I had asked for?

That same afternoon I was on the phone with my friend Peter Redgrove, and we were discussing our weekends.

"What did you do?" I asked.

"I went to Palm Springs. Something odd happened. Out of the blue, a friend of mine bought me a painting."

"Of what?" I asked.

"It was a picture entitled *Abraham Lincoln Freeing the Slaves*."

Lincoln again! It had to be another bit of proof. That evening, as I sat at my dining room table writing out some bills, I reached for my checkbook and accidentally brushed my wallet off the table. As I bent down to pick it up, Lincoln's eyes stared back at me. A five-dollar bill had fallen out of the wallet. *Okay, I get it*, I thought, and I thanked the powers that be for my proof.

Over the next few weeks, not a day went by without a reference to Lincoln. They were small, but I knew that the little things are often signs from the other side. I found a penny on the stage during one of my demonstrations. As I browsed through a bookstore, suddenly a biography of Lincoln fell off a shelf. Traveling to a dinner date with a friend in Santa Monica, I got off the wrong exit, looked up at the sign, and read: LINCOLN BOULEVARD!

The energy of Lincoln's message has stayed with me. Every day I thank him for being my guide. In fact, I carry a picture of him in my wallet as a reminder of my special mission and the power of his spiritual presence in my life.

Child Guides

Whenever I see spirit children, I know that they are on a very special mission. Many years ago, before I began my readings, I worked temporarily at Midway Hospital in Los Angeles as a clerk in the personnel department. I loved the job because my boss, Margaret Morgan, was a wonderful person. We would often joke around to make the day go by. One day Margaret asked me to bring some papers to the fourth-floor nursing station. I got into the elevator and pushed the fourth-floor button. For some reason, the elevator opened on the third floor. No one was around. Curious to see a floor I had never been on, I got off the elevator and walked down the main hallway. Halfway down, I noticed a group of laughing children enter one of the rooms. *How odd*, I thought, *for children to be walking around a hospital floor.* I wondered if I was on the children's ward. I followed the children down the hall, peeking into each room on my way. I realized that it was not the children's ward at all. All the occupants were elderly patients on the final leg of their journey. Most of them were hooked up to oxygen tanks and other lifesaving machines.

I stopped outside the room where the children had entered and looked in. An old woman struggled for breath, and the sound of her death rattle filled the room. The children reached out toward her with hands of golden light. It struck me that these children were spirit guides ready to assist the old woman out of the physical plane. I turned and walked back toward the elevators. I sat down at the end of the hallway and stared at the floor, trying to digest the thoughts that flooded my mind. Suddenly a high-pitched beep went off. Nurses, seemingly out of nowhere, rushed into the old woman's room. I knew that she was gone.

Children are indeed God's little angels. Many are exalted spiritual teachers who bring their energy of joy and amusement to earthly souls who have lost their own innocence and truth. Child guides help us to remember the fun of life and to keep our hearts and minds open to our blessings.

Angels

Angels are spiritual messengers and instruments of divine guidance, inspiration, and protection. Some of these divine beings have very specific work and are part of various kingdoms or specific realms, such as the Counselor realm, made up of Seraphim, Cherubim, and Thrones. The heavenly governors make up the second realm of Dominions, Virtues, and Powers, and the third realm consists of Principalities, Archangels, and Angels.

Although I do not see angels very frequently, I have called on the angelic kingdoms whenever I feel a need for some extra help. They have never let me down and have taught me valuable lessons in humility and faith.

I was in New York on a publicity tour for a television movie I had produced entitled *The Dead Will Tell*, starring Eva Longoria and Anne Heche. Somehow I had agreed to be a guest on Howard Stern's radio show. Although I had been invited on the show several times in the past, I always shied away. I knew that Howard was a stubborn skeptic of the paranormal, and I didn't want to endure his ridicule. Ironically, I had felt a kinship with

Howard. He had bucked the establishment and stayed true to himself, and I applaud anyone who prods others to question the norm while enduring public disapproval. Howard certainly did and continues to do it his way.

I was up at five in the morning, somewhat apprehensive and having second thoughts about going on the show. It was a good time to meditate. I asked my guides for divine protection. Immediately, a beautiful being with blond hair and blue eyes appeared. He wore a white tunic and purple robe with a golden sword strapped to his chest. I knew instantly that I was in the presence of the Archangel Michael. With one quick, downward stroke of his sword, I heard the words, *You are protected.* I opened my eyes and smiled. My fears had dissipated, and I headed out the door for the studio.

The moment I arrived I could see Howard standing at the coffee machine. He looked gargantuan, as if he were seven feet tall. I went up to him and introduced myself. Immediately I realized that Howard Stern is a down-to-earth guy and all his bravado is purely part of his public persona.

When we sat down in the studio, Howard looked over at me and said, "You know, I don't believe you can talk to the dead."

I heard the words coming out of my mouth before I could stop them. "I really don't care what you believe."

Howard smiled. At that moment, I knew we would get along, and the interview proceeded without Howard's usual embarrassing comments and disrespect. At the end, Howard asked if his girlfriend could meet me. "She loves this sort of thing."

So we never know how angels do their jobs. Our part is to surrender and let them do their work. Help is always available, but we must have the faith and courage to let it in.

You've just gotten a glimpse of the many dimensions that intertwine and exceed our own physical atmosphere and the beings that

inhabit these dimensions. As I have said many times to many audiences, just because we don't see these dimensions does not mean that they do not exist. Everything is part of the one energy source of spirit, no matter the rate of vibration or the form it takes. It is all energy.

SIX

Everything Is Energy

Have you ever had the feeling that someone was watching over you but you couldn't see who it was? Have you ever felt a cold chill run down your spine? Did you ever hear footsteps when no one was around? Or have you ever met someone for the first time and disliked him or her immediately? This feeling, this sensing—is it real? What exactly are these manifestations? The answer is simple: *energy*.

Simply put, energy is a force, or a relationship between two objects. It has a variety of different definitions. Some refer to energy as the life force of all thought and matter. Others think of energy as a magnetized element that holds all things together in our Universe. When I am asked to describe energy, I reply that energy is a combination of particles of molecules and electrons that behave in certain patterns. Everything is made from these particles; therefore everything is made of energy. The most important thing to remember about energy is that, depending on the dimension, these particles move at various rates of speed. For instance, the particles of matter that make up chairs, houses, trees, flowers, and your own physical body all move at a very slow rate of speed because they vibrate in a three-dimensional world. Ghosts vibrate at a higher rate because they are in a fourth dimension.

Suffice it to say, energy refers to many things that make our world work. There are different types of energy, such as electrical, mechanical, chemical, and thermal. The type of energy discussed in this chapter is kinetic, or spirit, energy.

THE LIGHT BEING

I had a very profound experience of spirit energy several years ago. I was in my office feeling pretty sorry for myself. Most of us have been in this kind of mood at some point in our lives, especially anyone who is very sensitive to the human condition. The unsettling feeling of global problems mixed with the ignorance and closed-mindedness of people in authority grinded away inside me. I sat there and reviewed my life wondering if I was doing enough to help change people's minds and attitudes. I wondered why I was able to peer into the dark parts of the planet. What did that say about me?

Suddenly I noticed out of the corner of my eye a light on the floor in the room. At first I thought it was a ray of sunlight, but looking out of the window, I saw only clouds. Then I felt an incredible sensation of heat behind me and turned around to look. I was in awe at what I saw. It was a being of some sort—its shape was not that of a human body. It did not feel either male or female; it seemed to be neutral in essence. It had no particular attributes like love or fear but was simply a steady energy. Suddenly I felt prompted to go to the mirror and take a good look at myself. I could hear words saying, in effect, *Sense your energy, see who you truly are, do not let your earthly mind distort the truth.* I glanced in the mirror and saw a bright green light emerging from the center of my chest. It was as if this light had been superimposed over me. The green was so vibrant, otherworldly, and indescribably beautiful that it brought tears to my eyes. At that moment, I became aware of my own compassion and immediately thought, *I don't need to hide my light under a bush just because there is such overwhelming cruelty in the world.*

It was a profound experience and reminded me once again of my spiritual heritage and my mission in life. I thought of the very first reading I ever did and the effect it had on another human being. I thought about my decision to give up a well-paying job with insurance and benefits and to take a leap of faith into the unknown to become a mouthpiece for the spirit world. I had always felt a loving energy from spirits, and it had changed my life. I knew this energy could change the life of anyone else as well.

On this particular day, I witnessed spirit energy in a completely different form from what I had been used to, but I knew it was still the great love that could heal the world. Since then, I have shared the "green light" in most of my healing meditations, and many people have told me, in person or by e-mail, that it was this green light healing meditation that gave them the awareness and understanding to deal with difficult issues and ultimately brought about profound changes in their lives.

SENSING ENERGY

Here is a very simple, quick, and safe way for you to experience what your own energy feels like. To begin, shake both arms away from your body. This helps you to loosen up and relax. Hold your hands in front of your body about two feet apart with your palms facing each other. Close your eyes and become completely and totally aware of nothing else but the space between the palms of your hands. After several seconds, slowly begin to move the palms of your hands toward one another. Pay attention to what happens in the space between your hands. As you slowly move your palms closer together, you will begin to feel a tingling sensation or magnetic force emanating from your palms. This sensation may remind you of the pull of two magnets when held opposite one another. As you bring your palms even closer together, you will feel a more pronounced tingling sensation. This is the feeling of energy. Become familiar with it so that you will be able to recognize the feeling. Play with this invisible energy as if you were playing with a ball. Push your palms together and away from each other as if you were playing an accordion. By now, you can tell that this energy, this force, is extremely subtle and sensitive. In order to perceive energy, you must become aware of the "lightness" of this force.

Another energy exercise I teach requires two people. Have your partner stand about three feet away from you with his back facing you. Ask your partner to close his eyes, relax, and tune in to his body and notice how it feels. Stand behind your partner and extend your hands with your palms facing your partner's back. Very slowly, make a pushing motion, moving your hands back and forth toward your partner's back. Be patient and keep it going. Within several minutes, you will notice that his body is beginning to sway back and forth in concert with the movement of your hands. You are manipulating the energy surrounding your partner (known as a person's aura) with the energy from your hands.

You don't need hands to send energy. You can also send energy with your thoughts, through your prayers and intentions. The energy of thought is called telepathy. How often have you thought about someone and five minutes later the person called you? You are using telepathic energy to connect with that person. Very often when people are ill we send prayers and good thoughts their way. By doing this, we are sending them positive energy. Thought energy is the fastest way to contact anyone living or dead.

Another exercise I use in my workshops has to do with picking up on someone else's energy—or, as the expression goes, "tuning in to another person's wavelength." I ask students to enter a meditative state so that they can become more neutral to their surroundings. Then I ask them to concentrate on an individual, first by visualizing that person's face as if he or she were right in front of them. Next, in their mind's eye, they must act as though they are standing with the person and discussing something in extreme detail. At the end of their conversation, they are to instruct the other person to call them. After this exercise, I tell students to wait twenty-four hours for the individual to contact them. When the person calls, they must ask the person why he or she called. It is so interesting to see whether their discussion in the meditation is what they will talk about.

On the second day of one workshop weekend, two of my students told me at the lunch break that that very morning they had received messages on their cell phones from the people about whom they were meditating. So, you see, it really does work.

This is one exercise that has changed many people's point of view about spirit energy and proven without a doubt that it is real. Depending on your ability to sense and control energy, you can begin to tune in to almost anything.

TUNING IN TO A GHOST'S ENERGY

Over the many years I have toured countries around the world, my psychic eyes have perceived energies both good and bad. When I see that a ghostly face has overshadowed a human face and the human has no idea of what's going on, having allowed a ghostly energy to enter into his or her space, I often want to shake that person awake. I am not afraid when I see these dark, unevolved spirits, but when they suddenly pop up out of the blue and surprise me, I feel as though I am the host of a Halloween party. That brings me to the following incident.

Just recently, I was on a ten-day workshop tour in Australia. I always enjoy my travels because I get to observe the diversity of people around the world. I always find that although people look different and speak in different languages, everyone is really quite similar. On one of my afternoons off, I headed for the Oxford section of Sydney to buy something new to wear for that evening's demonstration. My friends Ann and Peter joined me, and we strolled the area enjoying the sights and the variety of stores. We walked into a men's shop where I found a great pair of blue trousers. There was one problem. If I wanted to wear them that evening, I had to get them hemmed. The shop owner pointed in the direction of a nearby tailor, and off we went. As we headed down the street, I noticed a shoe store and suddenly shouted, "Here they are!" "They" were a pair of perfect sandals that Peter had been looking for to wear at tour's end at the Great Barrier Reef. The very tiny shoe store must have been all of two hundred square feet, and it was crowded with people. Peter tried on his sandals, and they fit perfectly. As he waited in line to pay the cashier, Ann and I browsed around.

Suddenly I started to get extremely uncomfortable and claustrophobic, as if the walls were closing in on me. I looked around for Ann, but she was on the other side of the shop, and several people stood between us. The feeling worsened, and I felt as if I were drowning and needed Ann to throw me a life preserver. I didn't know what was going on, but I was in heavy distress. I looked over at Peter to tell him that I was going outside to wait. Just then, the man in front of him finished his transaction and, with his bag of shoes in hand, turned to leave. Our eyes met, and I almost screamed. Looking at me, almost through me, was the face of a skeleton superimposed over this man's face. I felt very nauseated and knew I had to leave the store immediately. I grabbed Ann on my way out and told her what I had just observed. I kept pointing at the man who had left the store and was now halfway down the road. "He's possessed!" I told her.

Finally, Peter emerged from the store while I was still feeling the impact of the vision. He said to us, "Something is not very right in that store. I think it's a front for drugs."

"Really?" I replied.

"Yes, I could feel a lot of bad energy."

Then I told him what I had seen and how I had felt.

"That's what I felt too," Peter confirmed.

When we thought about it later, Peter, Ann, and I realized that the shoe store wasn't all that great, nor were the prices. Maybe Peter was right. Maybe there was something more in the back room besides shoes.

As we continued down the street, I suggested that we all do a certain exercise to eliminate whatever we might have picked up in the shoe store. Peter and Ann were only too happy to get rid of anything foreboding that might have attached to them. I had them imagine magnets attached to the soles of their feet. The magnets could pull any heavy, dark energy out of their bodies, through their feet, and straight into the earth. In the earth, this dark energy would be absorbed and neutralized. After this simple exercise, we all felt a little bit lighter and greatly relieved.

THE BODY'S ENERGY SYSTEM

By now, you are beginning to get the gist of what energy is and how we can sense it. I also want you to be aware of the energy system that works in the body itself. This energy is very akin to the motherboard or hard drive of a computer. Your body's energy system is made up of the energy that flows up and down your spine to various centers of your body. Each of these centers is a generator for a different part of the body. When there is a break in the flow of this energy through emotional, mental, or physical trauma, the energy will often decrease or get stuck. A lack of this vital force may later become an abnormality such as pain, discomfort, or disease. It's important to familiarize yourself with the body's energy-generating system, known as the seven main chakras or psychic centers. Each chakra spins like a swirling ball of colored light and corresponds to various parts of ourselves.

1. At the base of the spine is the first chakra, the root chakra. Being the energy closest to the earth, it is red, the color of earth. This chakra has to do with our survival instinct and basic physical needs. When we concentrate on the root chakra, we can pull the energy of the earth up through this center to give ourselves strength and vitality.

2. The next center is the sacral chakra, located two inches below the belly button around our pelvis. This area is our intuitive center. Because it is associated with our feelings and raw emotions, it is a source of clairsentience, or "clear feeling." It is associated with the color orange. Physically, this center corresponds to our sexual organs, spleen, and bladder and can be an emotional storage area for hurts.

3. The third chakra is about two inches above the navel in our solar plexus. This is where emotions are more refined. This chakra has to do with will and a sense of self. On the physical level, this chakra is associated with our stomach and digestion. It is also the emotional storage area for anger and repression. This yellow-colored chakra connects to the silver cord that tethers us to our bodies. When we sleep and dream, or astral-travel, we do so in our etheric bodies and are connected to our physical bodies through this silver cord. When we die, this cord snaps, our physical bodies die, and our spiritual bodies are free to move on.

4. Higher energy starts at the heart chakra. This center vibrates to the color green. Located in the center of the chest, it is associated with the heart, the thymus, and blood circulation. This is the center of love, compassion, trust, giving, receiving, and nurturing. When the heart chakra is blocked, a person may feel a lack of love for himself and others.

5. The throat chakra vibrates in the color blue and is located in the neck area. Through this chakra, along with the solar plexus and spleen chakras, mediums can hear the voices of ghosts, and ghosts can speak through channels with their actual voices. Physically, this is the center of our creative expression, our voice, throat, mouth, thyroid, and hypothalamus. Emotional problems that stick to this area usually pertain to feeling powerless in expressing our true selves.

6. The third-eye chakra is located in the center of the forehead and vibrates to the color indigo or dark blue. Focusing on the third eye chakra in meditation helps to develop spiritual awareness. This center, which is used to see auras and spirits, physically corresponds with our eyes and pineal and pituitary glands located in the brain. The "third eye" is the gateway to the spiritual realms.

7. The seventh or crown chakra vibrates at the top of and above our heads. This is the seat of spiritual consciousness, enlightenment, mysticism, and protection. Concentrate on the color purple when meditating on this chakra. Physically, it corresponds to our spinal column, central nervous system, and cerebral cortex. When working with spirits, it is a good idea to bring the light through this crown chakra down into our bodies to the root chakra in order to protect ourselves from unwanted energies.

SCANNING THE BODY

In 1989 I was about to begin a reading for a client named Judy when I noticed that she was uncontrollably nervous. Before I could continue I had to calm her down, so I guided her through a meditation. Then, as I scanned Judy's life force, I intuitively detected a blockage. I saw a brownish, gummy type of substance sticking to her uterus. It appeared to be what I call an emotional "knot." I knew immediately that Judy had some unresolved emotional issue and it was throwing her physical body off balance. Left untreated, this knot could eventually develop into some kind of cancer.

I asked Judy, "Have you ever had a pain or discomfort in this area?"

"Yes . . . occasionally, but I am not sure what it is."

I then asked her if she had ever lost a child and felt responsible for its loss.

Judy lowered her head and whispered, "Yes, it was a boy, and he died after three weeks." The doctors had told her the baby died of SIDS, or Sudden Infant Death Syndrome.

I explained to Judy, "The soul of your son is fine. It was part of his soul's evolution to go through that particular experience. You need to look at this experience differently. It was an opportunity for your son's soul to grow. You were a part of his spiritual learning experience, and you should not feel guilty. Guilt will only cause problems in your body."

Judy seemed to understand.

As I continued to explain about the relationship between souls and their growth, I noticed the brownish mass of corrosive energy in Judy's body begin to break apart and to dissipate. I could see her life force flow through that area, as it should. By the end of our meeting, Judy looked younger.

She told me, "I feel so energized. I haven't felt this way in a long time."

I smiled and wished her well on her path.

THE HEALING HOUSE

We have all had the experience of being around positive, loving people. It feels good just to be around them. When others are joyful, we feel happy too. An individual with thoughts of love and light draws other individuals who are like-minded and loving. It is difficult to always live in this manner because our physical world is filled with many challenges and obstacles to overcome. However, love is our natural state of being and the greatest force there is. It can overcome any darkness, imbalance, or disharmony. The more we make an effort to keep our thoughts positive, the more pleasurable our journey in life will be.

Through the years I have been so blessed to meet some incredible healers, spiritual teachers, and others who have revealed their truly heroic experiences. I always feel honored when they share their stories with me.

I would like to describe two particular instances that demonstrate how loving, positive energy resulted in the manifestation of some very highly evolved beings.

Lilia Begette was a Canadian homemaker and one of the most adorable and loving persons I have ever met. She seemed like a cross between Dr. Ruth and Yoda, standing five feet tall with a heart as big as her house. As a young woman, she used to read tea leaves for her girlfriends and was uncannily correct with her visions. Years later, after her husband died, Lilia felt a calling to do something bigger with her life, something that would have a profound impact on others. She moved to Fort Lauderdale and bought a house in a suburban neighborhood where she began to teach classes in metaphysics. During one class, Lilia's life changed forever. A spirit guide came to her and told her to prepare her house as a healing center. Lilia shared this message with her students and friends and soon began renovating her house. Walls were taken down to enlarge the rooms into huge healing spaces. One room was entirely decorated in pink, from the walls to the twelve beds that were covered with pink sheets and blankets. Lilia reserved her pink room for anyone who seemed to be having emotional problems. The energy in this pink room was that of complete and unconditional love. Another room was all decked out in green. This room was also set up with twelve beds, and everything in this room was green, a symbol of healing energy. Lilia felt that the vibration of a particular color drew the energy associated with that color into it, and she was absolutely right.

When I was fortunate enough to meet Lilia through my friend Pat, she was already eighty-one years young. I could sense her loving energy and very powerful psychic ability. We spoke for a while about our unique experiences with spiritual work and our philosophies on life and death. Lilia explained how she was guided to create her wonderful healing center.

"I can't explain what exactly happens in the rooms," she said. "I just tuck people in, say a prayer, and leave the rest to those upstairs. I want you both to experience the energy for yourselves."

Lilia led Pat and me upstairs to the green room. Two other people, a young woman and an older man, were already in their beds. Lilia told us to climb into bed and get comfortable while she checked on the other two across the room. I took off my shoes and got under the covers; I was ready to take a nap. Pat also got into bed and waited for Lilia. As I lay there, I looked over and noticed Lilia praying over the girl in bed. Then I turned my head and saw a long line of ghosts dressed in medical garb standing in the center of the room. I could not believe that I was seeing teams of ghost doctors and nurses. When Lilia had finished her prayers and moved on to the old man, a ghostly medical team went to work on the girl, administering healing energy. It was an unbelievable sight, and one that I wished everyone could see.

When Lilia came to my bed, I knew it was my turn. She murmured several prayers, but the only prayer I recognized was the "Our Father." Then she gently tucked me in and went to Pat. I closed my eyes. I wasn't sure if I wanted to see the medical team or not. Several moments later, I felt a warm glow around me and opened my eyes. The ghostly face of a doctor dressed in white looked back at me. Three others, a nurse and two other doctors, also dressed in white coats, accompanied him. The ghostly doctor had his hands around the back of my neck and seemed to be adjusting it. I immediately felt a change in my physical body. I closed my eyes to take it all in. I could feel the ghostly team touching my back and abdomen and my body moving up and down as some kind of adjustments were being made. I happened to look over at Pat, and her body was also moving up and down. At one point Pat sat up, then lay back down. As the team worked on me, I felt an incredible amount of peace, lightness, and balance throughout my body. I sensed that when they were finished I would know, so I closed my eyes and rested while the ghosts did their work. Twenty minutes later, Pat and I looked over at one another and knew we were done. The energy in the room had dissipated, and it was time to leave.

We sat in the living room and spoke to Lilia at length. Lilia told us, "I pray to set the energy in the room so that healing can take place. My intention is to welcome healers to use the space I have created."

I looked at Lilia and said, "It works."

TO SAVE THEIR SONS

A similar experience happened recently during a healing week-end retreat in Mount Shasta, California. Two fathers, Raoul and Jorge, had traveled all the way from Colombia in South America to this particular event. They shared many things in common. They were brothers-in-law who lived in the same town, and both had a son who had died tragically. They felt that this was perhaps their best chance to see if at least one of their sons would come through and communicate with them. As the message part of my seminar got under way, my spirit guides quickly brought me over to Raoul. Next to him, I saw his son very clearly. Half his head had been blown off. Ghosts will often show me their death expe-riences, and when I see gunshot wounds or burned flesh, the vi-sions can be very disturbing.

I asked Raoul, "Was your son shot in a car?"

Raoul quickly responded, "Yes."

His son was telling me, *My father needs to be fixed*. Looking at the son, who was dripping with blood, I would have thought the opposite.

As I continued, Jorge's son also appeared. Unlike the other boy, he didn't demonstrate his death condition to me. Instead, I saw a body covered with tattoos that made him look rather menacing.

I asked Jorge, "Was your son a member of a gang?"

Jorge replied, "Yes."

Jorge's son was chewing gum with an attitude. He didn't appear to be at all remorseful. I could tell that he still held on to his gang mentality. It seemed that he was killed by a rival gang member, so I asked him if he was.

His response was, *Yeah, I had it coming to me!*

Jorge acknowledged the message. His head sank down, and he mumbled to himself something that was unintelligible to me.

The other ghost with the bleeding head looked at me and said, *Help my dad, please. He feels so guilty.*

I asked Raoul, "Do you feel responsible for your son's death?"

"Yes."

I explained to Raoul, "You had nothing to do with your boy's passing."

Raoul could not be convinced. He would not accept freedom from his guilt.

Suddenly three spirit doctors appeared. They looked like a surgery team. One doctor with white hair and deep blue eyes put his hand up toward me, as if to tell me to stop the message part of the reading so that they could help. They impressed upon me that I needed to get everyone's attention while they focused on Raoul. I explained to everyone that a team of spirit doctors had come to heal Raoul, and then I stopped speaking and let the doctors do their work. The spirits proceeded to the area of Raoul's intestines. I could see tightness there. In fact, his entire stomach was matted with dark brown and black spots.

To validate their finding, the white-haired doctor asked me to check with Raoul about any recent trouble with digestion.

Raoul concurred. "Yes, I have been having pains in my stomach."

The spirit team then performed surgery on Raoul. I could see in his etheric body that his second and third chakras had become putrefied by the guilt he felt over his son's death.

Everyone was quiet as the team of doctors removed the emotional garbage from Raoul's stomach. I watched in amazement. They were done in about five minutes. I noticed that Raoul's son had also changed. Instead of a bloody head, I saw a tall, brown-eyed young man who was very much at peace. It was a poignant sight to see. This experience also demonstrated to me what can happen to our energetic bodies if we don't resolve various emotional upsets.

At the end of the event, I did a book signing, and the two South American fathers came over to the table. I noticed that their boys stood on either side of them. Gone were the dripping blood and half-shot-off head. Raoul's boy wore a bright white shirt, and he had a smile to match. All the love that emanated from him showed me that he was very proud of his father. Jorge's son, the one once covered in tattoos, showed me his arms. As his spirit body transformed right before me, the tattoos disappeared, his weight increased, and his hair grew back. He also had a bright smile and a sparkle in his eyes. The old gum-chewing, gang attitude had vanished. Instead, he pointed at me and giggled, as if we were all a part of some cosmic joke.

At that moment, Jorge said, "Thank you, James. I no longer think of my son as dead."

WHEN GHOSTS DRAIN YOUR ENERGY

If there are energy healers, it stands to reason that there are also energy drainers. Energy suckers are everywhere, and I am not just talking about ghosts. Is there someone in your life who is constantly depressed, angry about the world, jealous, always in a bad mood, pessimistic, doubtful, power-hungry, mistrustful, or manipulating? I refer to these individuals as "psychic vampires" because they unconsciously drain your life force with their unrelentingly negative attitudes. Most of them are not even aware that their energy extends beyond them and hurts others along their path. They can leave you exhausted, depressed, and debilitated.

Psychic vampires usually are self-involved individuals who feel self-important. Their bad attitudes actually slow down their vibratory rates and attract unevolved ghostly energies. Ghosts can draw energy from electrical items such as televisions, radios, microwaves, lights, and phones by pulling energy from the electromagnetic field surrounding these objects. Unfortunately, appliances don't hold enough charge, so ghosts must seek energy from somewhere else. The most energy possible comes from the living. That means *you!* The human body has the exact type of electrical circuitry that is familiar to a ghost, and so it's easy for a ghost to plug into our energy and take it. They do so through the holes and leaks that appear in an individual's chakra system when it has been weakened and depleted by negative thoughts, feelings, and behavior.

When ghostly energies attach to humans, they can be very scary, as I saw in the shoe store in Sydney. *The Ghost Whisperer* doesn't even come close to depicting some of the darker forces I have seen. You would be shocked to know that many people who behave in horrific ways are being impressed or even possessed by dark and unevolved entities. Ghosts that attach to humans simply drain energy. Any form of chronic poor health can be a sign of ghostly attachment. Unfortunately, those with ghostly attachments don't relate any of these ills to their own negative mindset. However, ghostly attachments can drain energy to the point of causing the living to suffer accidents, injuries, and other misfortunes.

THAT'S SHOWBIZ!

As you know, I have worked for many years in television as an on-air talent and producer. I have met some incredibly nice, light, wonderful, and loving Hollywood personalities, executives, and crew members. At the same time, it is impossible for a psychic like me to wait in studios, agent offices, and TV executive suites and not witness many disturbing scenes involving Hollywood's most celebrated people. Many have risen to the top with driving energies that are mean-spirited and malevolent. To them, it doesn't matter how they got to their position or what they have to do to stay there. They have very little integrity or mutual respect for other human beings. Their lives are all about their lust for power and ego gratification. Power might come to them—but often at a very high cost.

When I was a child, I loved the musical *Damn Yankees* about a major league baseball player who makes a deal with the devil so that his team, the Washington Senators, will win the pennant. It's the old Mephistopheles concept of selling your soul to the devil for something you greatly desire. I am not sure if I liked the music or the idea more, but the show really grabbed my interest. Hollywood reminds me very much of *Damn Yankees*. So many will sell their souls, identities, and morality to gain power, unaware that they have started a fire that in time will burn out of control. The need for power is created by fear. Fear can be a great motivator, but it also can be one of the greatest destructive forces we know.

Whenever I have to go somewhere in Hollywood where a lot of people are gathered, whether it's an award show, dinner, or TV set, I use a series of meditative and visualization exercises before I go out the door. I have found that this ritual protects me from any wandering ghosts, lower elementals, or stray thought forms that might be looking for a place to attach themselves. As I have said repeatedly in all my books, like attracts like, and if you are a good person, nothing of a lower nature should bother you. However, when walking among Hollywood's insecure personalities, you can never have enough protection. The protection ritual takes about five minutes, and on this particular day I was so happy I had done it because what I was about to experience was really bad.

At one major studio, there was a completely unscrupulous producer working on a TV show. He was in the habit of lying to everyone in order to get what he wanted, always using the excuse, "It's what's best for the show." However, he really only wanted what was best for him. If that meant someone else would have to get fired or take the blame, then so be it. There were many people on the set who would have given their blood, sweat, and tears to make the show work, and this producer was the type who would take all the credit. I am sure many of you have worked for someone just like him: a boss whose reality is based on selfishness and manipulation.

On this particular day, I was in my office going over some production notes. When I had a question for one of the staff members, I left my office and walked down the hall toward the other end of the floor. Halfway down, I stopped in my tracks because an overwhelmingly bad odor had gotten my immediate attention. It smelled like sulfur or rotting eggs.

"Hey, James, how's it going?" I turned to see this very same arrogant producer behind me. I promptly moved over to let him pass. Just feeling his energy made my skin crawl. For me, the image that came closest to describing his energy was that of the character Pig Pen from Charles Schultz's *Peanuts* comics. Pig Pen is the one with a big ball of dirt around him. I could not believe what I was seeing. Dark, dirty shadows and snakelike creatures protruded from the top of this producer's head. It was like watching a real-life Medusa walk by. Looking at his back, I saw various shapes and sizes of what appeared to be knives or swords. He looked like a porcupine. What quickly came to mind about the swords was that they might be negative thought forms sent by people he had wronged in the past. These negative energies were actually living on his back. I could not wait to get out of there, so I turned around and went straight back to my office to write down what I had witnessed.

It was obvious that this producer had no clue about the negative thought forms he was carrying on his back. Those negative energies would probably not have a completely physical effect on him for several more years, but who can say. The more bad behavior he engaged in and the more jealousy and insensitivity he showed toward others, the more life and power these attachments would probably accumulate. A persistently negative mindset can open a person to something far worse, and that is possession.

POSSESSION

Who can forget the movie *The Exorcist*, starring Linda Blair? After seeing it, I couldn't sleep for weeks without having the lights on. Ironically, I read William Peter Blatty's book when I was in the seminary studying to be a priest. Interesting, isn't it! Anyway, in the movie the young girl, Regan (played by Linda Blair), is possessed by a demon. Her entire personality changes, and she is unrecognizable even by her own mother (played by Ellen Burstyn). Of course, this movie was made purely for entertainment value, so the scary parts were a bit over the top and much more dramatic than any actual possession I have ever witnessed. However, even though possession might not include chucking up green pea soup, spirit energies can indeed come into a person's sphere and influence him or her in a very negative way. In fact, most possessions are so subtle that it is sometimes difficult to believe that a person is behaving any differently than normal—probably because that person's "normal," like the TV producer I just described, is negative in the first place.

Alcohol and drug abusers, who continuously use substances, are perfect targets for unevolved ghostly energies. Ghosts take over these people just to experience once again the physical satisfactions and highs they left behind. We've all heard the expression "he is not himself when he is drinking." It has more meaning than you think. An alcoholic who has been influenced by a ghost isn't himself. A ghost has taken over his energy and is in the driver's seat.

Possession happens more frequently than we are aware of. I believe murderers, rapists, and molesters fit into this category as well. I have seen many people who are so enraged that they are completely under the influence of one or two ghosts.

When O. J. Simpson was on trial for murder, I had a distinct sense that he was influenced and possessed by a lower-level entity. So, when he says he wasn't there, he wasn't there on a conscious level. Another part, the possessed part, took over. Perhaps the entity entered his energy field and took over after Simpson got loaded and fell asleep on his couch. I have noticed that he is still surrounded by unevolved ghosts, and he is still struggling with these demons. I predict that his life will come to a violent end.

Possession does not excuse anyone's actions, because a person has to be in a base state before possession can take place. Most of us have nothing to worry about because we are good, loving people and have a natural defense system made with our loving thoughts and deeds. But the others . . . ?

We have all been to places that we find disturbing, unsafe, or threatening. Perhaps it was skid row, or a very crowded bar, or a hospital, or even prison. We come away from these places feeling bad and usually don't know why. It is the same with people. Most of us have been around negative people who tend to bring us down, and we walk away from these people feeling depressed or irritated. We may not know why certain people or places cause temporary physical, emotional, or mental reactions, but we feel them nevertheless. It is because we were born with an innate sense (our sixth sense) of the energy that surrounds us.

Each day you are bombarded with energy. A tremendous amount of this energy consists of the leftover mental thoughts that people have had. These thoughts attract a multitude of ghosts to us or dispel them away from us. For instance, let's say that someone has an ongoing drug problem or has been in a deep depression for many years. That energy attracts low-level ghosts who feed off heavy, depressing, negative energy. If they can, they will attach to such a person and siphon off all that negative energy, building up more and more of this type of energy.

That's why there are certain places and areas in our cities inhabited by dozens and dozens of low-level ghosts. You might say that these places are powerful epicenters of negative energy. These ghosts can have varying degrees of influence over the living, ranging from mild energy drain to extremely rare total possession.

Some of the telltale signs that low-level ghosts may be hanging around include:

- Hearing voices

- Sudden cravings for alcohol, cigarettes, and drugs, especially after surgery or a traumatic event

- Sudden weight gain, especially after surgery or a traumatic event

- Fears and phobias

- Sudden changes in behavior, such as increased anger, depression, or thoughts of suicide

- Serious illness of unknown cause

- Loss of energy

- Memory and concentration problems

- Unexplained physical problems—such as pain from an undetermined cause

- Migraine headaches

- Night terrors and nightmares

- Panic or anxiety attacks

- Multiple personalities

Most of us are safe from attachments by negative ghosts, but as you can see, we should be aware of their existence because anyone can come under their influence now and then. Who is vulnerable to attachments? First of all, those who don't take good care of their health. Second, those who are addicted to drugs and alcohol on a daily basis. Finally, those who have a mind-set of control over others and anger toward others, like gangbangers. These people are predisposed to negative influences.

Your aura is your natural defense against such intrusions. By keeping your aura strong, you ensure that lower-frequency spirits cannot attach to you. I scan my body on a daily basis to make sure my own energy is strong. I often imagine a green light coming from my heart in front of me and all around me. This green light represents healing and love. With my mind, I make my intention: I am in the perfect state of health and filled with love. This is the easiest way to ensure that there are no negative hangers-on in my space.

So the next time you walk to work, stop, turn, and look all around you. Be aware of your environment. Do you feel a cold chill hitting your cheek? Do you hear something that is not there? Become aware of the energy around you. It can have an effect on your body, your mind, and your general outlook on life.

Start now to change your life in significant ways. Become a lot more cautious with your thoughts, both the ones you send out to others and the ones you verbalize. Be more concerned about whom you befriend and where you hang out, where you work, the type of work you do, and even where you live.

Remember, there are a lot of energies, both living and dead, of which you need to be aware because not all of them are working in your best interest. The next time you have a weird and unsettling feeling about a person or place, pay attention, surround yourself with light, and walk quickly away from that person or place. It is up to you to protect yourself from unwanted energies.

Not all ghosts are negative. Some ghosts are more than willing to be helpful influences in our lives. The way to attract these spirits is with our own good energy.

SEVEN

How Ghosts Communicate

It takes a lot of energy for a ghost to make something manifest on the physical level. That's where we come in. The more willing we are to open ourselves to the existence of ghosts and to educate ourselves about their ability to communicate, the more ghosts will reveal themselves to us. Ghosts attempt to reach us in a variety of ways, including through temperature changes; knocking sounds; familiar, identifiable scents such as perfume or tobacco; and changes in the electricity in our lights, radios, televisions, phones, and so on. They manipulate matter and energy by moving things around, by getting information to us through people or animals, and by leading us off the beaten path. Ghosts will use anything to get our attention. I am constantly amazed when people share their own personal experiences of ghostly encounters because it is almost always something new to me. Ghosts are inventive, and because they are not bound by physical nature, their ingenuity is limitless.

Evelyn, a woman at one of my workshops, once told me that after her father died she would notice when she visited her mother that the house her parents had lived in for thirty years still smelled of stale tobacco from all the years of her father's smoking.

"I told my mother to get the drapes and rugs cleaned to eliminate cigarette odor. She did. She even gave away my father's clothes and threw out all the ashtrays. Yet every time I went to visit there was the telltale smell of tobacco."

"Was he a heavy smoker?" I asked.

"He smoked from the age of nine. There was never a time I saw him without a cigarette dangling from his mouth. Burns and stains were everywhere—on the carpet, on the furniture—and he must have had a hole in every shirt he wore just from falling ashes. The only time he stopped smoking was when the doctor told him he had lung cancer."

"So you think the cigarette smell was your father?"

"Well, not at first. I just thought that the smoke had gotten into everything. But after the carpet and drapes were cleaned and the smell was still there, I knew it had to be him."

"Is he still there now?"

"No, the aroma left about a year after he died. I think he just wanted to stay around to see that my mom was okay."

SHOW US A SIGN

Why do ghosts want to communicate with us? Ghosts are just like us, and their reasons vary, but it seems that the most common reason a ghost wants to communicate is to help the grieving family. Soon after a person passes over to the other side, he or she feels the pain and suffering of family members in mourning. A ghost wants nothing more than to let the family know that he or she is *not dead* but very much alive, and so the ghost stays very close by. Most families are in so deep a state of shock, or so caught up in the funeral ritual, that they don't realize their loved one is right there shouting out to them. It is as if someone is calling on the phone and, instead of answering it, we just let it ring and ring. Ghosts feel great frustration when they can't get through to their loved ones.

Like most children who lose a parent, my sister Lynn and I were extremely upset, but we knew, of course, that our father was around us. I had seen him several times at the funeral home and received many reassuring messages. However, Lynn had not. The day had come to put my father's house up for sale, and Lynn and I went inside to say our last good-byes to our childhood memories. We walked through the house one room at a time, and in each room we reminisced about a certain time. We laughed and cried as our memories danced before us.

When we walked into our parents' bedroom, Lynn and I instantly smelled the distinctive and familiar scent of Old Spice aftershave. It was our dad's favorite, and we both clutched at one another and yelled out, "Do you smell that?" There was no mistaking that recognizably strong aroma. Even though I did not see his ghostly figure at that particular moment, I knew he was trying to reassure us that he was there. After thirty minutes, we knew it was time to put the old memories to rest. We left the house.

Lynn said to me as we got into the car, "Jamie, I hope we are doing the right thing." Then she looked up to the sky and petitioned, "Dad, please just give us a sign that it's all right with you that we sell your house."

Although I am the medium, Lynn does have a lot of psychic ability, and her intuition is quite powerful. She is very talented in saying something and, whatever it is, having it occur. As we drove away from our house, Lynn insisted, "I bet you he will give us a sign that it's okay to sell the house." Ten minutes later, as we turned left onto Northern Boulevard in Queens, Lynn got her sign. She excitedly shrieked, "Oh, my God, there it is! It's Dad!" Lynn pointed at the car in front of us. The license plate read

"AVP–770K." My father's first name was Allan. Allan Van Praagh. His initials were AVP, the same as on the license plate.

Like the license plate, signs aren't always what we expect them to be. It depends on how a ghost is able to get his or her point across. Many times ghostly signs are subtle but recognizable. Often they seem like coincidences. Letting go of rational thinking and tuning in to our intuitive minds is more difficult if we do not make a constant practice of it. However, the more open we become, the more often we will recognize our loved ones' contact with us.

THE EXTRA

Please remember, ghosts have the same mind-set they had on earth. If they were stubborn here, they're stubborn still. They won't give up until they are heard.

During the second season of *The Ghost Whisperer*, I was on the set observing. I am there primarily to help answer any questions that Jennifer Love Hewitt, the star of the show, might have regarding the way her character would react in a certain ghostly situation. This day's scene took place in the village square, and there were many extras on the set. As I looked at the crowd, something caught my eye. A blond female extra, about thirty-five years old, crossed the street, and I noticed an older woman with dirty blond hair in a blue sweater mimicking the young woman's every step. The older woman was a ghost. I was amused by the older woman trying to get the young woman's attention. The ghost tapped the young woman on the shoulder, she blew into her ear, she mussed up her hair, but none of these things worked. The young woman, like most of us, was oblivious to what was going on because she could not see it with her own two eyes. At some point, the ghost yelled into her face, but to no avail. I could sense that the ghost had something she wanted to communicate and was getting mighty frustrated. I watched this scene repeat itself about half a dozen times. I knew the extra was totally clueless, as most of us are.

Eventually, the assistant director yelled, "Cut," and the crew broke for lunch. All the extras went to the holding pen to line up at the food truck. At that moment, I felt obligated to help the blond extra, so I walked over to her table and introduced myself.

She looked up at me and was practically speechless. "I'm such a big fan of yours," she told me. "It's such an honor just working on this show. You know, it's so weird that you came over to me. It must mean something, don't you think?"

"It might," I replied. "Can we go over there and sit down under the tree?" I asked as I pointed to an unoccupied corner of the set.

Surprised by my offer, she quickly responded, "Of course."

After we sat on a bench, she introduced herself. "I'm Donna, by the way."

The ghost who had been there earlier appeared right in front of me. She made some sort of hand gestures. *Tell her it's not her fault.*

I told Donna what I had witnessed for the past hour, and she began to cry. She seemed quite upset by my description, and I wasn't sure that I had done the right thing by giving her the ghost's message. However, I know it's not my place to pass judgment one way or the other. My job is to give the message, so I continued.

"She is telling me that it wasn't your fault. Do you understand?"

Donna continued to sob, and the ghost began to rub Donna's shoulders. Donna looked up at me with tear-filled eyes and slowly began to explain what the message meant.

"My mother, Sheila, had been in and out of the hospital for a year with bone cancer. It was terminal, and she suffered so much."

I sat there and empathized with her.

"Toward the end, she fell into a coma, and I would visit her every day. It was so hard to see her life slowly drift away. I knew she was in pain because she was on a morphine drip by then."

Donna explained that she wanted her mother to die with some dignity. "One evening I went into her room and whispered into her ear, 'It's okay to go home now. I'll be all right. I want you to be at peace.'"

Donna told the doctors to take her mother off the respirator, and within two hours Sheila died.

"Ever since then, I've lived with regret and guilt. What if I did the wrong thing? Who am I to tell them to pull the plug? My brother, Jack, still accuses me of murdering my mother."

Sheila began to speak to me through my thoughts. I told Donna what her mother wanted her to know. "She is telling me that you did the right thing for her. It was an act of love. She cannot thank you enough. Your motivation was pure," I said to Donna. "You meant to help her, not hurt her."

Donna wiped away her tears.

"Your mother is saying that she has been trying to contact you for the past year. Do you have a lamp on the table to the left of the bed?"

"Yes," she responded.

"Your mother has been working very hard to manipulate the electricity by making the lightbulb go on and off all the time."

"I thought there was a short in the lamp, so I unplugged it."

"Your mother says that she even moved things around in your room, like books. Have things been disappearing? She is saying that she moved a picture of her that you had on the nightstand."

Donna's eyes opened wide. "That was her! I didn't know what happened to the picture and was afraid I knocked it into the trash can by mistake. I was wondering why weird things were happening."

"Now she is telling me something about the laundry room."

"Oh, my goodness, I found the picture on a shelf in the laundry room and wondered how in the world it got there."

"She also tells me you misplace your keys a lot."

"Yes, I do, James. This is remarkable. I even made a joke to my mother to give them back."

"Well, Sheila tells me she moves them around a lot."

"Why does she do that?" Donna asked.

"She is trying to slow you down and get your attention. You keep busy, and you worry too much. She wants you to spend time enjoying yourself."

Donna agreed and then started to laugh.

"Your mother is here because she cannot move on without your help. You have to let go of all the guilt you feel. You did nothing wrong," I said.

Then Sheila told me about a book.

"There's a book next to your bed with gold lettering," I said to Donna. "It fell off the table today."

"Yes . . . yes, it did!" Donna started crying again. She shook her head from side to side, murmuring, "I can't believe this."

I reassured her that it was all right and gave her a hug.

Donna looked into my eyes. "James, the name of the book she is referring to is *Letting Go*. My mother was reading the book in the hospital. Now that I think about it, the book has fallen off the table at least twice, especially when I was really having a hard time. I thought my mom was angry with me. I am so happy to know that she isn't."

Sheila kept talking about other members of the family. I could see the relief in Donna's whole demeanor. She was finally free of her guilty feelings.

No one on the set even knew what had transpired between Donna, her mother, and me and the beautiful message of love and forgiveness that we all shared.

I often say that there are no accidents. I was meant to be on the set that day. I had to help Donna. The spirit world will often give what I call "validation signs" that we are in the right place at the right time doing the right thing. My validation sign came that very day when I realized that the episode we were shooting was about a family having to make the decision whether or not to pull the plug on a young man in a coma. A coincidence? I don't think so.

I'LL SEE YOU IN MY DREAMS

Without a doubt, the easiest way to hear from a loved one is through our dreams. I often ask people in my demonstrations, "How many of you have dreamed of a loved one who has passed over?" Ninety percent of the people raise their hands. Some have a better recall of their dreams than others. Remembering dreams is merely a matter of practice.

Dream visitations are quite common. In the sleep state, our minds are no longer conscious and rational; the intuitive, subconscious mind is in control. Therefore, the defense mechanism that prohibits us from accepting the unseen world is asleep, and we are unfettered and free to be open to the other dimensions. Many have described their dream visits as very real; there is a sense that they are occurring in a tangible setting and that the conversation is genuine. These visitations have also been described as warnings: a ghost reveals some prophetic information about approaching danger. Many times dreams are symbolic and we have to examine the dream meaning as thoroughly as we can to ascertain its significance.

My aunt Anne McLane was the second-oldest of eight children. The family was very close. Gradually, one by one, Aunt Anne's brothers and sisters passed away. No wonder I talk to the dead, I joke with my audience. When I was a child, I used to attend one funeral a year. It was called "the Irish Curse," as my mother's side of the family was Irish. But funerals were also occasions when the whole family would get together for a family reunion, which I always thought was weird.

Anne was the last surviving sister, and she lived alone in a craftsman-style house in Mount Morris, New York, a small, depressed town that had seen better days. My aunt was a special lady; she had a faith in God and the Catholic Church like no one I had ever met. Anne was independent and unique. She certainly did things her way and had a natural curiosity about the world and people. She was sweet and delightful, with always a kind word to say, and she would put others at ease by making them feel special in some way.

Unfortunately, in her later years she suffered a lot from arthritis and had a difficult time getting around. Nevertheless, she would still say, "Jamie, if God gave me this cross to bear, then that is what I have to deal with. There are a lot of people who have it a lot worse."

I never really discussed in detail my line of work because Aunt Anne was a true Catholic believer, and talking to the dead didn't fit into her belief system. I respected her and didn't want to disturb her beliefs. Only after Freddie, her husband of fifty-two years, had passed over did we even bring the subject up. She seemed more than a little curious about what happens when we go to heaven.

Several years back, I called my ninety-year-old Aunt Anne, and we spoke for a while. It was the last phone conversation I had with her. She told me about a dream she'd had the night before.

"I was a young girl sitting on the porch of the house where we all grew up. All of my brothers and sisters were walking down the sidewalk, and some were far off in the distance. Suddenly I looked up and saw my mother reaching out her hand to me. 'Come on, Anne,' she said, 'you're always lagging behind.'"

My aunt didn't understand what the dream meant, but I knew that her mother was coming to get her. A few months later, Anne died peacefully in her sleep.

A CRUISE TO TAHITI

I am so fortunate to be able to do the work I do. I help people to liberate their minds and let go of the fear of death. There is no greater personal reward for me than to truly make a positive difference in someone's life.

For many years I have taught classes all over the world, but I have found that one of the best ways to teach and see the world (and unpack only once) is on a cruise. In the early 1990s, I became friends with Ron Oyer, who was trying to increase his travel business. He came up with the idea of my doing a spiritual cruise, and thus the "Voyage of Enlightenment" began. Since our initial sailing, we must have done at least twelve cruises, and now other speakers and companies are taking advantage of Ron's incredible professionalism. He has become the go-to guy for these types of adventures.

One of our adventures took us to the enchanted land of Tahiti, located in French Polynesia. I tell people all the time that Tahiti is the closest thing to heaven that I can imagine. The blue-green colors, the hospitable locals, and the magical energy of the island make it a perfect place to do spiritual retreats.

At our orientation breakfast, I discussed with the group the process of talking to ghosts. I explained that in order to have the best possible results, they had to let go of any expectations they might have brought with them.

Expectations often block any chance for communication. I liken expectations to a garden hose that has been twisted over and over again. Water cannot pass through it because the flow has been stopped. To remain open while expecting something to

happen can be a daunting task. Everyone wants immediate gratification, especially if they are paying for it. I remind people, however, that ghosts manifest in many subtle ways. They might come
through me, or a message might come from another person in the
room. Ghosts might even manifest through someone totally un-
related to the workshop itself.

Such was the case with Joyce Randall. Joyce had taken our trip
to Tahiti after the devastating death of her daughter Marie. Marie
was a vibrant, young premed student. As Joyce told me, "Marie
had always wanted to be a doctor since she was a little girl." Unfortunately, Marie's life was cut short by a rare bone disease.

Joyce was shy and unassuming, and she really was at a loss
when her daughter died. She had been in an emotional tailspin
and was anxious to make contact with her daughter. After getting to know Joyce, it became apparent that this mother-daugh-
ter relationship was atypical. It was obvious that Joyce had been
the child and Marie had been the parent who took care of her
mother emotionally and psychologically. With her daughter gone,
Joyce's life was also taken away. She didn't know how to handle
her grief. Then one day a friend of hers gave her my book *Healing
Grief*, and she went on my Web site and booked the trip.

This was Joyce's first cruise. As she explained, "I never went
anyplace by myself before." This cruise turned out to be an experience that would change Joyce's life forever. During the week,
Joyce would come to me and tell me lovely stories about her
daughter. Each memory carried with it a tear. She wished that in
some small way she could recapture some part of her past. I
looked into her eyes and felt her suffering. She seemed very depressed and quite alone. "I am sure your daughter will reveal herself in some way. Just be open to the signs." Joyce would nod her
head and go on her way.

One day we had arranged to have a special workshop on land
hosted by a native of the island. The talk was on Tahitian culture

and spiritual beliefs. Joyce went to the workshop. "I'm not sure why I'm here, but I just felt I should come," she said to me when she arrived. Then she turned and looked at the native woman hosting the workshop and her jaw dropped open. "That's Marie," she squealed. "She's the spitting image of my daughter." When she found out that the host's name was Maria and that her birthday was only two days away from her daughter's, Joyce was ecstatic.

For her part, the host, Maria, knew that the moment she saw Joyce there was an instant connection between them. I might add that Maria's mother had recently passed. Maria and Joyce both realized that the spirit world had played a part in bringing them together in a way neither could have ever imagined. Joyce and Maria have continued to correspond with each other through phone calls, e-mails, and letters. They remind each other that no one is ever lost or forgotten and that the love between mother and daughter is always present.

A BIRTHDAY SURPRISE

Another way spirits make contact with us is through photography. I have seen many photographs showing white orbs or what look like wisps of smoke around figures in a photo. Many people think their photos have been ruined. However, I believe that somehow ghosts have impressed a portion of their energy on the electromagnetic energy of the photograph. Again, it takes a lot of ghostly energy to do this, but I have an entire page of my Web site dedicated to "phantom" photographs.

My brother-in-law Dennis left by suicide over ten years ago, and months after his death I did a reading for my niece Gail. Dennis had always been skeptical of mediums and communication with ghosts, so when he came through in the reading, I was a bit surprised. One of the first things he admitted was, *I'm alive, and I can speak to you.* After communicating some touching messages to his daughter, Dennis ended by saying, *I'll see you all at the birthday party.*

I was sure that he meant Gail's birthday, which was only a few days away, but her birthday came and went, and nothing happened. Gail and I were both disappointed.

Three months after the reading, Dennis's granddaughter Brittany turned three. The next day, my sister Lynn called me and practically screamed on the phone, "You're never gonna believe this!"

"What?" I asked.

"Dennis! He showed up in the picture with Brittany! He is kneeling down and reaching his hand toward her."

"You're kidding." But I knew that Lynn wasn't joking.

About a month after our phone conversation, I met my sister in New York, and she showed me the photograph. I have to say, it remains to this day the clearest spirit photograph I have ever seen. Not only were his nose and eyes apparent, but I could also make out his sideburns, body, shirt, and pants.

Dennis proved to everyone—but I think mostly to himself—that there is indeed life beyond death.

OUR SON THE GEOLOGIST

There are times when a ghost employs a unique and rare method of communication through the manipulation of molecular structure. In other words, a ghost can make an object appear or disappear. A ghost is also able to move an object from one part of a room to another, or to another room entirely. It takes a lot of energy to do this, but it is real, and it does happen.

In August 2001, we had chartered the sailing vessel *Wind Spirit* for a cruise from Turkey to Athens. Water is a very special conductor of energy; as a result, the experiences people have on our

cruises are often amplified in one way or another. This particular
workshop brought together people from all parts of the world
and all walks of life. We had a few medical professionals, a homemaker, and even a newlywed couple, to name a few. All had one
goal—to have an experience that would transform their lives.

Fayed and Shania, a married couple from Kuwait, had lost
their son Bruno about a year before. They took the cruise in the
hope of contacting him and getting closure. Bruno had loved
everything about rocks and had studied geology in college. At the
young age of twenty-four, Bruno was very well respected by his
colleagues for his intelligence and talent.

As with all of my workshops, I explained to the audience how
the process of ghostly communication works. After doing ap-
proximately twelve readings that first session, I felt that I had relayed all of the messages that needed to be given, and we ended
for the day. Fayed and Shania were disappointed that Bruno did
not come through. Everyone went to their rooms to dress for
dinner except Fayed and Shania. They stayed behind, grieving
tearfully for their young son.

My assistant Jorge was still in the room putting things away,
and he could tell that the couple was quite upset. He explained
again what I had said in the workshop. "Just because James didn't
bring you a message from your son doesn't mean your son's not
around. Be open. Something will happen to let you know that he
is here with you. Something always happens in these workshops."
Fayed and Shania felt comforted by Jorge's words and returned
to their stateroom to prepare for dinner.

As Fayed was washing up in the bathroom, he reached for a
hand towel. Suddenly a large rock fell to the floor. He screamed
for his wife to come and look. Shania rushed into the bathroom
and saw Fayed staring at the rock on the floor. "What is it?" she
asked.

"It's Bruno!" Fayed said excitedly. "The rock came from Bruno. He left us a rock in the middle of our room in the middle of the sea."

Fayed and Shania came to dinner, their auras lit up in gold and blue colors, and I knew something had happened. When they told me about the rock from nowhere, I was totally blown away by the materialization. To this day I think it was one of the strongest examples I have ever witnessed of the power of ghostly communication.

Ghosts have an impact on us more often with their thoughts and actions than we could ever imagine. Even the word *inspiration* actually means "in spirit." Because we cannot apply physical laws of time and space to the spiritual worlds, often what we label as coincidence is really the influence of the spirit world. We need to be more inquisitive about our coincidences, as there is no such thing as accident or luck. Our Universe, although perceived by many as chaotic and out of control, is a perfectly run system governed by spiritual laws. The next time a coincidence occurs in your life, investigate it and dig a little deeper into what it might mean. There is always something underneath a chance meeting or a lucky break. Usually, it is a ghost or two trying to send us a message.

Please remember that a ghost in the light will communicate in a nonthreatening way. An earthbound ghost, however, is more likely to be distressed or confused and will communicate by causing disturbances. It is the earthbound ghost that haunts the living and is apt to cause harm.

EIGHT

Some Go Haunting

I'm going to freeze to death! I thought to myself as my teeth chattered and my hands and feet grew numb from the cold. Even rubbing my hands together couldn't bring any feeling back. I could not help berating myself, *Gee, James, why didn't you wear your overcoat before running out the door? Why did you go in this damn broom closet in the first place? Why did you have to be so nosy? I wonder if anyone else sees them? What do they want? Why won't they leave me alone!* I started to shake, not from the cold, but from fear. I was scared, very scared.

That cold November night in the outdoor broom closet was not the first time I had hidden away. The routine seemed to be happening a lot. I wanted to tell someone about the things that I could see. I don't know why I didn't, but in a way it was "our" secret, and I felt that if I had disclosed what I saw, I might be harmed in some way. No one else was able to see what I could, and half of the time the other kids thought I was just plain crazy. Hiding was my only solace.

Suddenly the door to the outdoor closet opened.

"What in the world are you doing in here? You could have frozen to death!" Brother Martin shouted. "Now get to the dorm and make your bed. Hurry up!"

It was seven in the morning. I must have dozed off between the brooms and the rakes. I was fourteen years old and a student at Eymard Catholic Preparatory Seminary. Instead of attending high school, I had decided to become a priest. I was still not sure about my decision, but I thought if I could go to school in a beautiful setting instead of being stuck in a filthy city, then I was all for it. Eymard Seminary was in a pristine location along the Hudson River in Hyde Park, New York. The Franklin D. Roosevelt Library bordered it on the south, and the Vanderbilt Mansion sat at the northern edge of the property. Actually, the seminary was once the Vanderbilts' hunting lodge.

The moment my father and mother dropped me off at Eymard that first Sunday in September 1972 I knew something didn't feel right. As soon as my eyes gazed upon the facade of the mammoth stone structure, I felt as if I were choking. Suddenly I heard a woman's piercing scream. I turned to my parents and pleaded, "I changed my mind. I don't want to go here anymore."

"Do you know the sacrifices we made in order for you to attend this school?" my father said. My mother did her best to calm me. "It's normal to feel scared the first time you leave home."

"Okay," I said with some hesitation. I just had to suck it up.

The inside of the mansion was just as menacing as the outside. It looked like something right out of a Vincent Price horror movie, only it wasn't a movie set and I had to live in it. As I walked around the main foyer, I noticed floor-to-ceiling stained-glass windows that cast colorful shadows on the highly polished, rich mahogany floor. The walls were paneled in dark wood. A wide, wooden staircase loomed over the center of the foyer. I could imagine the owners making a regal entrance as they walked down the stairs to the waiting guests below. I felt as if the hunting lodge was a museum consumed by an overwhelming sense of sadness.

The brothers came out to greet the freshman group and to escort us to a third-floor dormitory. As we ascended the massive staircase, I noticed that the walls were carved in scenes of hunters cutting the hides of their fresh kills. Perfect. At the top of the first floor was a statue of the Blessed Virgin Mary. It seemed so out of place in this house of horrors. I looked over the stairs at the living room below and saw three shadowy figures flee into an adjacent room. I stopped in my tracks and stared.

"Keep moving, James," said Brother Joe. He grabbed my hand and pulled me up the steps.

"Who are those people?" I asked.

"What people?"

"The lady in a gray dress and a young boy. They were walking in the back of the living room."

Brother Joe ushered the other boys into the dormitory. Then he bent down and said in a hushed but firm tone, "This is a place of God. We don't allow any nonsense here. You make sure to keep your thoughts holy. Get in your room."

I entered the dorm. It was basically a long hall extending the length of the house with several side rooms and bathrooms. It looked like a converted attic.

"Hi, I'm James," I said to a few of the boys. They just nodded and grunted "hi" back. I noticed that I was the shortest one there, so I felt awkward and somewhat self-conscious. My bed was at the end of the hall on the right. Steve was in the bed next to me. At first, Steve was nice to me, but as time went by he would join a clique and his attitude toward me would change.

I unpacked my bags and unhappily sat on my bed. All of a sudden, I had an urge to walk to the other end of the hallway. Halfway down, I passed a room and felt something strange. I looked in. Immediately, I heard that same piercing scream I had heard when I arrived. This time I could make out some words. *Please . . . help him . . . you're killing him . . . stop!* The voice got so loud that I had to bend down and cover my ears.

This was not a good way to start school. I was very impressionable, and this impression would last until I left the seminary. The room contained five beds and seemed normal enough except that it was circular. There was a balcony that had been converted into a fire escape. The sign on the balcony read, UNDER NO CIRCUMSTANCES IS THIS TO BE OPEN. I wondered whether that included when there was a fire as well.

I returned to my bed to unpack the rest of my things. I knew that I was in a strange and uneasy setting, and deep down I also knew that there was a ghost (or ghosts) haunting this place and that whoever it was didn't seem to be very nice. To top it off, I had a horrible sense that someone was watching me because he knew I could see him.

The next morning I woke up and felt something touch my neck. I screamed, "Aaaahhh!" I reached up and felt what seemed to be strands of hair and began to cry. Suddenly a roar of laughter filled the room. I opened my eyes and saw a stringy mop lying next to me. I was a victim of a not-very-amusing practical joke. These kids who were supposedly going to be future priests acted more like inmates in a reform school. Then it dawned on me. These kids weren't holy. They were problem kids whose parents sent them to this seminary hoping the brothers could reform them and make them into good Catholic young men.

After that incident, my feelings of isolation and insecurity increased. I always had an uneasy sense that someone's eyes were trailing my every step, and this menacing energy seemed to be getting stronger. I could feel that this ghost was on the verge of making itself known.

After several weeks, a rumor began to go around that someone was breaking into the wine cellar and destroying the wine bottles. One day during morning Mass we all heard the sound of shattering glass. A few priests jumped to attention and ran behind the altar. Mass concluded about a half hour later, and as we silently walked toward the dining room the sound of a siren broke the quietness. During breakfast, Brother Robert came to tell us that Father John, one of the priests who had run to investigate the sounds behind the altar, had experienced chest pains and been taken to the hospital. When we asked him about the crashing sound, he said, "Some mice got into the wine." I thought to myself, *They must have been some pretty strong mice.*

When Father John returned to the seminary, he never spoke about the time he went to investigate the sound behind the altar. Looking back at that experience, and at all the other odd things that happened in the seminary, I realized that the brothers and priests knew the place was haunted. In fact, one evening when I walked by the priests' dining room and overheard them arguing, one of the older priests was saying, "They can get the hell out. It isn't their home anymore!" Of course, no one ever talked about ghosts. It was a sin for Catholics to believe in such things.

Several times throughout my first year there were a series of accidents and close calls. One kid almost overdosed in the basement on water purification tablets. Several seminarians were expelled for violent attacks that seemed to be over nothing. School was becoming an extremely tense place to be, at least for me.

As more things happened, my dreams got more vivid. In one dream, the sound of whimpering and coughing was coming from one of the far bedrooms. I entered the room and saw a man dressed in an old pair of overalls and a dirty white shirt. A young boy about seven years old was lying on the floor coughing and looking extremely pale. I noticed that there was something in the man's hands. As he turned to look at me, I saw that he had a knife and a rope. I knew that he was preparing a noose to put around the boy's neck. When I looked at the man, he said, *Get out of here. This is none of your business!* The window next to him suddenly flew open, and I awakened in a pool of sweat. The dream was so real that I ran to Brother Robert's room and banged on his door to tell him my story. He patted me on the head. "It's just a nightmare. Many of the boys have them. You're far from your home and family. Go back to bed. Everything is all right." Unfortunately, the nightmares persisted, and although they were different, they were always about a man, a boy, and a lady, the latter two always running down the stairs screaming.

I had most of my visions in the evening, either during Mass or right before bed. During Mass, I would see a ghost priest saying Mass alongside the living priest. The ghost had different vestments, old-fashioned ones from an earlier period in time. Many times during Mass we heard strange sounds, or things would fall over without any rhyme or reason.

I remember one evening very distinctly. It was eight fifteen, and I was on a break. I was walking from the study hall, which was situated below the church, to the floor above. I saw a golden hue behind the muted glass doors of the church entrance. I opened the doors and saw the lady in a gray dress and a little boy push a candle in front of the Virgin Mary statue. The ghostly lady looked at me and started screaming, *I'm going to get you!* I freaked out and ran to the brother in study hall and explained what I had just seen. He ran up the stairs and grabbed a fire extinguisher. He thought I meant the church was on fire.

Soon other kids had similar weird dreams about a screaming woman, a priest, a man, a noose, and a small child. One night as we all walked into our dorm, Tom, one of our classmates, was in the corner kneeling on the floor, crying, "Don't kill him."

Tom told us, "There's a man putting a rope around a little boy's neck. He's going to hang him. We have to stop him."

That was enough for me. Tom confirmed my belief that the place was indeed haunted.

One afternoon the brothers invited the town historian to speak at a school assembly. All of the students sat in the auditorium eager to hear the gossip. Back in the early 1800s, before the Vanderbilts arrived, there was a family by the name of Smithers. The father, Jonathan, and the mother, Bessie, had a young son, Jules, who was very sick with tuberculosis. Apparently, they were very religious and superstitious people. Bessie called the local priest and told him that her son was possessed. She asked the priest to exorcise the devil from her sick son. The priest did his best to pray for the little boy. Jonathan didn't like the priest and thought he was only making things worse. As the young boy took a turn for the worse, his parents became despondent. Bessie cursed God for making her baby boy sick. Meanwhile, her husband's behavior grew more bizarre with each passing day. He stopped doing all his chores and let the farm fall into disarray. Bessie suspected that the priest had released the devil out of her son and into her husband.

Meanwhile, demented Jonathan plotted to get rid of the devil by killing his son and ending his suffering. One day he made a noose, placed it around the boy's neck, and hung his child out the window. Bessie came into the room and screamed, "Stop!" She pleaded as she grabbed for the rope. The rope snapped, and her little boy hung to death right in front of her eyes. Jonathan was so disturbed that he leaped out the window to his own death.

My guess now is that Bessie haunted the house because she wanted the priests and brothers to leave. She blamed the priest and the church for the deaths of her son and husband.

After that first year, I left the seminary and was happy to be back in public school. The enrollment in the seminary dropped from forty to ten students. After a few more years, the seminary closed its doors forever. Two years ago, I was in the very same area doing a workshop. I drove by the old mansion. The place was completely fenced off, but I could see the house from a distance. As I

was looking at it, I had the feeling that the place was still not free
of ghostly activity. It just didn't feel clean. A neighbor walked over
to me to inquire about my curiosity.

"I used to go here when I was in high school."

"You're not the first one," he replied. "Many of the former students have come back here to look at the old place, just to see if
it's still standing."

"What do they think?" I asked.

"They all have a strange reaction when they look over there.
Some loved it, and others would never step foot in there again."

The neighbor walked away.

I got back in my car and drove away. My only hope was that
one day the ghosts haunting there would cross over into the light
and find peace.

WHAT IS A HAUNTING?

My experience in the seminary is a perfect example of ghosts
haunting a familiar place. In my opinion, most places are haunted
in one way or another. We may not be aware of the various entities that travel alongside us, but ghosts can freely roam anywhere
they choose because, as I have said, they are not limited by the
physical dimension. They don't need any form of transportation
to get from one place to another because they travel by thought.
In the astral realms, everything is sharper and clearer, and a
ghost's memories are very vivid.

A haunted place is any area with a high concentration of
ghostly activity that lasts over a prolonged period of time. Based
on my investigations, I have found that these places have a strong
emotional tie for the ghost. Like the seminary that was haunted
by its past occupants, there are very strong mental and emotional
memories associated with the place, and the ghosts either want to
somehow relive these memories or cannot stop reliving them.

That is when ghosts cause disturbances in the energy. On the other hand, ghosts may just want to watch over a place and make sure the new occupants respect their home and take care of it the way they once did.

DESILU STUDIOS

It is quite common for ghosts to haunt their previous work environments. I have personally communicated with many ghosts who liked their work so much and spent so much of their time and energy at work that they often went back to visit. One of the most famous ghosts who still hangs out at her place of work is Lucille Ball. She has communicated with me on two separate occasions. The first time I met Lucy was during a segment for CBS's *Entertainment Tonight*. I hosted a tour around the Paramount Studios lot to locate ghosts from Hollywood's past heyday. Several famous ghosts did make themselves known, but none as famous as the comic redhead herself.

Lucille Ball told me, *I was working all the time and missed my kids.* She decided to make the Desilu studios "kid-friendly" and let the employees bring their children to work. Because of her clout, Lucy was the first to create a day care center in a studio. She also told me, *I would plan picnics and parties all the time for the employees and their kids. It was the mother in me.* As she spoke, I communicated our conversation to the camera. Then Lucy pointed in the direction of her personal apartment.

Come on, I'll show you, she said.

The crew and I walked toward a building that presently housed a TV production company. The office assistant behind a desk looked startled to see the camera guys and soundman invading the entrance.

"Hi," I said, shaking his hand. "We're doing a piece for *Entertainment Tonight.*"

As the cameraman took shots of the area, I told the assistant, "I'm a medium, and I am communicating with the ghost of Lucille Ball. She is telling me that she had a room in the back. She would go back there and lie down on the couch. Do you know what I mean?"

Shocked, the young kid replied, "Ah, yes. That was Lucy's private living room, and she supposedly used to go back there and rest."

Lucy made it very clear to me: *I'm not resting anymore.* I told the office worker, "You know, Lucy comes around all the time."

The redhead went on to say that she had spent so many tedious hours designing her apartment. *Now it looks so blah,* she said sadly.

As we walked around the offices, Lucy continued. *I horse around with the current occupants. It's my way of having fun. Sometimes I'll just knock some papers off the desk and open and close the door to the office.*

As proof of this, I asked the office worker if such things had occurred. The young man was a little spooked by the information. He nervously chuckled and agreed. "Yes, papers do fly off my desk for no reason, and there have been occasions when the door would open by itself, and no one is here but me."

"It's Lucy!" I told him with excitement in my voice. "She comes here to check on the studio that she helped build. She is saying that she has had so many happy memories here."

With her own unique flare, Lucy ended the conversation. *Why wouldn't I come back here to relive the best years of my life?*

Although ghosts usually frequent places connected to their past, I have also found that some haunt a place to which they have no emotional ties. Sometimes ghosts choose a particular environment—whether a place, an experience, or a person—because something about it calls to them. On the other hand, they may have wanted to be a part of a particular environment when alive but were never given the opportunity.

For instance, there are many ghosts who have always had the desire to be onstage, so they haunt a theater to "live out" that experience. Ghosts may also be fans of a particular actor, so they hang out with that actor to fulfill that desire. I have several acting clients who frequently tell me that there are always ghosts around them. When I ask a ghost why he or she does this, the reply is usually, *I'm here to help so-and-so with her part.*

I have communicated with ghosts who had been quite patriotic, and when they passed over, they headed straight to where the military was fighting in order to help the troops. It was their way of being of service to their country.

GHOSTS GO CLUBBING

Earthbound ghosts often go to places where there is an abundance of human energy. The first place that quickly comes to mind is a bar or club where alcohol is served. It seems that the more wasted the clientele is, the more easily ghosts can attach themselves. As mentioned, individuals in an inebriated state are susceptible to ghostly attachments because alcohol depletes their protective auric field. It's like letting down their guard.

I remember several years ago when I was in Minneapolis for a demonstration. After it was over, I thought I could unwind with a drink at one of the local bars. First of all, let me point out that anytime I am in an unfamiliar city I always do my protection ritual, because I never know if ghosts will be lurking about. The hotel concierge gave Kelley, my assistant, the name of a popular local bar that was a special hangout on Sunday nights. As Kelley and I walked to the bar, we noticed many boarded-up buildings; with a scarcity of stores, the streets were dimly lit. I said to Kelley, "I feel very weird. The energy around here feels dark and eerie. Make sure you build a wall of protection around yourself."

The instant Kelley and I walked into the club we were hit by the negative energy. The smell of mold and bleach filled the air and our nostrils. "This place is a pit," I said. With each step we took to the second floor, I felt worse. When we reached the dance floor, neither of us could see much through the flashing spotlights and neon signs. People seemed to be in a frenzied state as they tried to capture the rhythm of the blasting beat.

Although seeing people was difficult, seeing ghosts was not. The place was filled with them. Dark shadows followed people around, and dark figures crowded into corners. Some ghosts sat alongside people at the bar enjoying the pleasures of vodka martinis and tequila shots. Then I saw something I had never seen before. Sitting in a booth on the other side of the room was a very intoxicated young woman leaning over a table. Two ghosts sat next to her, one on each side. One was a skinny young woman who seemed to be high on drugs, and the other was a man who reminded me of a burned-out rocker.

I looked over at Kelley and said, "Okay, five minutes, and we're out of here." People were so drunk that several of them bumped into me on my way to find some ventilation. We didn't wait the five minutes. I looked at Kelley, and she looked back at me, and we made a beeline down the stairs. As we rushed out the door and felt the cool evening air, we felt a bit of relief. Then we turned and saw a long line of people waiting to get in. Several ghosts tagged along with the waiting customers. The whole atmosphere was a scary movie in the making. Kelley and I, both of us "creeped out" by the negative energy, quickly turned the corner and walked down the street as fast as we could. I said, "I feel as though I need a shower." Kelley replied, "Me too." At that very moment, it started to sprinkle. We laughed at the irony but kept walking. There was no hiding under awnings or in doorways in this neighborhood, not with such bad energy hanging around the entire area.

All I can say is that it felt like drug energy. Everyone who walked by us seemed to be strung out on something. When we were about three blocks away from the hotel, a crazed guy suddenly jumped out of an alley and screamed profanities at Kelley. We ran those final few blocks until we reached the safety of our hotel.

MORE GHOSTLY HANGOUTS

Besides bars, clubs, restaurants, theaters, and so on, ghosts also prey on humans who have a lot of "fear" energy. Fear, worry, and anxiousness are all emotions that attract earthbound ghosts. Ghosts feed on these emotions and, in turn, use them to build up their own energy. There are several places that contain fearful energy. What are these places? Believe it or not, dentists' offices are commonly filled with ghosts. Personally, I am not afraid of dentists, but whenever I go I keep a watchful eye out for ghosts lurking in a corner or two.

Other places that are surprisingly attractive to ghosts are law firms and courtrooms. Ghosts frequent these places because of all the fearful emotions attached to these areas. People in these settings are in distress, angry, wrongly accused, or perpetrators of crimes. Some ghosts may have been in trouble with the law when they were alive and cannot get enough of this type of energy. Some may have been innocent and want to see that justice is done.

Hospitals are another very big draw for ghosts. Hospitals are filled with sickness, worry, and the fear of death. Whenever I visit people in hospitals, ghosts are always milling around. Some are there to siphon off energy from people in weakened states. Others may be standing by to assist loved ones pass over to the other side. Then there are some ghosts who are newly dead and somewhat confused as to their whereabouts.

GHOSTS ON PLANES

Airplanes are another source of ghostly interference. I do understand ghosts on planes because, like me, many people are not good flyers. It's understandable that people have a fear of flying, especially since 9/11. However, many of the spirits I have seen on planes are not necessarily there to steal energy. Instead, they are on board to watch over loved ones who are afraid of flying. I know that several of my spirit guides accompany me to calm my fear of flying.

A few years back I was in the Memphis airport waiting to board a flight back home to Los Angeles. As I looked around the crowd at the gate, I saw a number of spirits around their loved ones. I didn't feel any bad energy from them, but one ghost in particular got my attention. He was rather tall and slightly plump. He wore a white shirt, blue jeans, and large, black sunglasses. He hung around a very pretty blonde and kept petting the top of her head. I wondered if he actually knew her or was just attracted, as a ghost, to her bright and friendly energy. The more I looked at this ghost, the more familiar he seemed. It crossed my mind that it might be Elvis, but I quickly discounted the idea because I was certain that I would easily recognize Elvis. I continued to rack my brain to fit a name to the face, but without much luck. Several minutes later, the gate attendant announced that it was time to board.

Since I was lucky enough to be in first class, I was one of the first people on the plane. I sat in my seat and made myself comfortable. Following right behind me was the very pretty blonde with the nice energy. She sat down in the seat next to me. We quickly introduced ourselves. The lovely woman was named Barbara, and she told me that she was a widow. I was happy that she did not recognize me because we spent the next couple of hours having a wonderful and enlightening conversation about life in Los Angeles, traveling, business, and family. Several times throughout our conversation, I noticed that the ghost with the black sunglasses stood right behind her. I didn't let on that I could see him, but I was still bothered by the fact that his face was so familiar. By the time we arrived in L.A., Barbara had told me what I had wanted to know all along. "I just came from the house my husband built in Memphis. He was Roy Orbison."

"Oh, my God!" I said. So that was who had been standing behind her! No wonder he looked so familiar. I never told Barbara the type of work I did, but I was happy to know that Roy was still around his "Pretty Woman."

PLACE MEMORY HAUNTING

Just like people, places can hold energy. This phenomenon is known as "place memory." It is a common type of haunting that is not well understood. It differs from the hauntings that I have previously discussed. Place memory is not only about ghosts having strong emotional connections to familiar places but about particular places holding an imprint or a recording of their history. Ghosts tend to get lost in these places and to reexperience a particular event or moment over and over again.

In my book *Heaven and Earth*, I wrote extensively about my "place memory" experience in Dallas. I was traveling by car and suddenly felt a shooting pain in my head. I told the driver, "Stop the car!" When I got out, I stood right in front of the book depository where President Kennedy was shot. Historic sites often have a role in this place type of memory haunting. Just as people hold on to memories, places hold memories too. It is the energy in historic sites or places where significant events occurred, like the book depository and streets of Dallas, that holds the memory of the incident that took place there. The event had an intense emotional component, and therefore the memory lingers on.

Battlefields are areas of strong place memories. People who visit these sites often feel the emotions that were present during combat. I have been told that you can hear soldiers crying out or feel the presence of gunfire in the atmosphere. One can't help but get caught up in this type of energy field and feel strange sensations.

THE ANNE FRANK HOUSE

In 1994 I took a trip to Europe, first to spend time with relatives in Wales, and then to visit the land of my ancestors in Holland. I arrived in Amsterdam on a very rainy Tuesday afternoon. I remember it well because it was very cold and I could not wait to get to my hotel and get into a warm bed. The next day was quite the opposite experience. The city was lit up like a Dutch painting. Everything and every place glistened from the golden rays of the sun: the bicycles, the distinctive canals, and the grand Dutch architecture. Amsterdam, one of the most charming cities I have ever been to in my life, is filled with place memory hauntings. I spent the day visiting the usual tourist sites, but there was one in particular that I had wanted to see for a very long time: the Anne Frank House.

I'd had a very strong identity with this house since I was a boy. I have long suspected that this identity stemmed from a memory of a past life, because I have always been fascinated by World War II. In high school I was involved in a production of the play *The Diary of Anne Frank.* I played the part of Mr. Dussel, the dentist who lived in hiding along with the Franks. Mr. Dussel was one of the most emotional characters I ever performed. I recall that on the first day of rehearsal, when I opened my mouth to recite my lines, a strong, deep, and powerful voice came through. I was shocked, as was everyone else in the room.

Even the teacher asked me, "How did you do that?"

"I don't know," I replied. "It just came out of me."

As I stood in front of the Frank House, I began to feel a very eerie sensation. I looked at the canal in front and thought, *This canal, this bridge, even the trees, are all exactly the way they were fifty years ago.* What had they witnessed? Suddenly, in my mind's eye, I was back in time. I saw German soldiers on motorbikes driving over the canals. I heard the shrill sounds of soldiers screaming in German for people to get out of their houses and move on and lots of gunshots in the distance. I felt frightened and alone and wanted to cry.

"Next please!" the ticket taker at the doorway announced as he held out his hand for my ticket. I quickly snapped back to present-day consciousness but could not shake the eerie and isolated impression still inside me. The tour guide explained that the Franks hid for two years in the annex above Mr. Frank's office. As I looked around the entryway, I could tell that things had been changed over the past fifty years and that none of the original belongings were there. Instead, there was current information about the house, the war, and human rights issues.

The official part of the tour began when the guide led us down a short hallway to a bookcase. I was in awe. Here was the original bookcase that had blocked the passage to the Franks's hiding place. Seeing the bookcase made the event very real and tangible. It was inspiring and at the same time sad. This commonplace bookcase was the only thing between the Nazis and the group of people who safely hid behind it for two long years. We were not allowed to take photos, but I could not help it. I whipped out my camera and snapped a picture before anyone noticed. I felt such a connection to this bookcase and this place. Maybe it was because of the play I was in long ago, but I could not stop thinking about Anne and her father, Otto, and the other family members. Anne may have fantasized about being a famous Hollywood actress, but did this little Dutch girl ever imagine that her life would become the stuff of books and movies and that her experience would change the world's understanding of the war? Her life played a much richer and more poignant part in history than would ever have happened from any role she might have played onstage.

As we climbed the stairs to the annex, I noticed that the walls had not been painted; they were exactly as they had been when the Franks lived there some fifty years earlier. I stopped and stared at a pencil mark. Had Anne drawn something on the wall, or did her pencil scrape the wall as she passed by? When we reached the top, only a few naked lightbulbs hung in the annex. As I walked around, I felt an overwhelming sense of being trapped. I couldn't breathe. The tour guide helped me to a seat in the doorway. The rest of the people continued through the different rooms while I caught my breath.

I noticed a piece of glass covering the original floral wallpaper, which had since faded. All of Anne's family photos, plus pictures that she had cut out from celebrity magazines of that period, were encased under glass. As I studied the photos, a man suddenly walked by. He was tall, with light brown hair, and he wore brown pants with suspenders and a white sleeveless undershirt. A towel over his bare shoulder suggested that he was on his way to or from the bathroom. As he passed, I telepathically asked, *Who are you?* He didn't take notice of me, but I heard the word *Fritz* in my head, and then he was gone. I had seen and felt enough for the day, and it was time for me to leave.

I walked downstairs to the museum area and perused the glass cases that housed various pieces of clothing from the concentration camps, dishes the Franks actually used, and more photographs of the annex occupants. As I walked around, taking it all in, it suddenly dawned on me. Standing next to Otto Frank in one of the photos was the man I saw upstairs. The caption listed him as Mr. Friedich "Fritz" Pfeiffer, also known as "Mr. Dussel."

I don't know why, but I hurriedly left the house and sat down on a bench by the canal. I said a prayer for "Mr. Dussel," the rest of the occupants of the annex, and the millions of souls who had had to experience such great tragedy. "May only light and happy memories be with them wherever they are."

I'm sure many of you have felt some kind of connection to past events, historical figures, or certain places. Being sensitive to the world around you and using your intuition are the primary ways to tune in to the spirit world. However, if you need additional help, there are a variety of methods that can speed up the process.

NINE

Making Contact

So far, this book has focused on ghosts—who they are, how they haunt, where they hang out, and how they try to get your attention. Perhaps your curiosity is ripe by now and you have a desire to explore the ghostly world on your own. Do you really want to see, feel, and communicate with ghosts? Is there a way you can enter this world?

Although I have my own particular method of contacting spirits, there are a number of ways and means to call upon and contact the ghostly regions. Some are simple enough and require little, if any, preparation. Other methods require a thought-out plan and some type of apparatus. I suggest that you study each technique and decide which one feels right for you. Some ways can take a lot of time and devotion, but remember: the end result may be worth it.

GHOST HUNTERS

By television standards, it seems like the world is more haunted nowadays. People are just plain curious about ghosts. You would not believe the number of ghost shows that are in development at production companies, never mind the Web sites dedicated to the subject matter, such as International Ghost Hunters, National Ghost Hunters, and any local town's Ghostbusters R Us. Besides TV ghost series like *The Ghost Whisperer*, ghosts seem to pop up on cop, medical, and law shows and in other network series. It's no wonder that a variety of ghostly reality TV shows have joined the bandwagon.

In these ghost-hunting reality shows, ordinary people seek out ghosts in haunted places and convey their findings on camera. Of course, these shows have a variety of specialists who claim to recognize ghostly apparitions. I am not sure what qualifications these specialists possess, or whether they can really detect dimensions where ghosts reside, but the shows are extremely popular. From my understanding, the stars of one show are plumbers by day and ghostbusters by night. I am sure they take their work very seriously, and I respect them for opening people's minds to the world of ghosts.

Today's technology has certainly made hunting ghosts more popular than ever before. Gone are the days of table tipping and flying sheets. Now we have not only night vision goggles but ghost-vision goggles, temperature recorders, energy receivers, sound amplifiers, and a potpourri of other instrumentation. If you want to go on your own ghost-hunting expedition and contact spirits in the manner of a ghostbuster, you will need the following ingredients.

Intention

There is one factor that I cannot emphasize enough, and that is the motive behind your desire to contact ghosts. You must have a clear intention as to why you want to explore this world. Do you want to be of service and help another person find his or her deceased relative or friend? Do you want to bring peace to a ghost? Are you helping a spirit move on? Do you want to rescue a ghost from its current troubled condition? Are you trying to contact the other side as a game, as a joke, or to scare your friends? Ghost hunting must be taken seriously because ghosts are *not* to be fooled with. You could very well enter a world for which you are not at all prepared, and there may be consequences you cannot handle. Remember that ghosts can read your mind and recognize your fear, and if you don't respect them by entering their world with knowledge and preparation, the results can have dire physical, mental, and emotional effects on you and anyone with you. This is not a game. You can be a beacon of understanding and a help to those who are lost, but only if you enter the astral dimensions with love and compassion for all those you contact.

Permission

Before working on any property, whether a house or other type of building, get the written permission of the owner, whether that party is an individual, a city, or the homeowners' association of a condo development. You must have permission to enter the property with the purpose of investigating paranormal activity.

Familiarize yourself with the history of the property, including previous owners, deeds of trust, builders, contractors who may have done additions and improvements, and the current owners. Research any and all records associated with the property. Find out whether there was another structure on the property before the current one. Research public records and newspapers to find out whether any significant incidents have taken place on the property, such as fires, murders, suicides, or other crimes. Remember that most hauntings are associated with past events that happened in a particular place. If possible, consider acquainting yourself with the property by visiting it several times, especially the night before your investigation. It is easier to investigate a place once you know its layout.

Equipment

Some basic equipment is needed for any ghost-hunting scenario. The following list will vary, depending on the sophistication of the organization or group involved.

- A watch
- A cell phone
- A notebook
- A thermometer or infrared thermal scanner to measure any environmental changes
- A Polaroid camera, a 35mm camera with high-speed film, and a digital camera
- A video camera and tripod (you don't want to hold the video camera all night)
- A natural electromagnetic field meter
- Digital and audiotape voice recorders (for interviews and Electronic Voice Phenomenon)
- A Geiger counter to measurer radiations leaks
- Thermal video monitors, which measure small changes in temperature and may show you ghosts on the monitor (very extravagant, but if you want to do it right, why not?)
- Audio amplifiers, which some ghost hunters believe enable you to hear EVPs (Electronic Voice Phenomena) better, though in urban areas with a lot of white noise it may be

difficult to differentiate what you are hearing (I don't recommend this equipment)

- First-aid kit

Preparation

You must know what you're looking for. What kind of activity is occurring on the property? If you are searching for a ghost or poltergeist, does it relate to a specific period of the past? Do you want to communicate with a relative or friend of the current owner? Before you begin, make sure you have a checklist to help you keep track of the following preparations:

- Never go on a ghost hunt alone. Have at least one other person along to assist you.

- Before you enter the property or start any work with the paranormal, always begin with a prayer of protection.

- Make sure that all of the equipment you will be using is fully charged and that you have extra fully charged batteries. Remember that ghosts feed on electrical energy.

- Set up a central location inside the house for storage of all equipment, batteries, and flashlights.

- Always carry a camera and flashlight on you; again, have extra batteries.

- Log significant conditions in your notebook, such as the weather or the electrical condition of the room or building.

- Allow only those people who are seriously interested in the project to be part of the investigation. Don't let strangers onto the property.

- If you have a large group, split into two so that each group can investigate different areas of the property.

- Record any and all activity, including meter abnormalities, strange sounds, spontaneous lights, and anxious or fearful emotional feelings of the group.

- Constantly check the equipment to make sure it is still working.

- Be respectful of the dead as well as the living who are on-site. Go with your gut. If you don't feel safe, leave immediately.

- When you are about to leave, say a closing protective prayer to bless yourself, the others with you, and any ghosts you may have encountered.

Investigation

If you decide to contact spirits in the ghost-hunter method described here, please remember that much of your success will rest on how completely you understand the process, including all the technical and paranormal terms. Also, you may not get the explanations you think you want because you are dealing with an entirely different dimension. Make sure to question everything you experience, and run it by the others who are taking part in the investigation. Make sure that everyone is on the same team and that someone with experience is involved. Do not ghost-hunt with just anyone. This is serious work.

When you research a paranormal organization, make sure it has the qualifications relevant to your investigation. Are the people involved professional investigators, or is the organization someone's part-time hobby? Does the organization have some sort of accreditation from the scientific community? How long has it been in business? What has been its history? Has it been successful in contacting ghosts and spirits? How much evidence has it collected?

Finally, what is the organization's reason for being involved in this work? Intention is important. Ask questions. Anyone nowadays can go out with a camera and audio equipment and say he or she is a ghost hunter. If you are investing time and money in this process, be sure to employ the genuine article. The people you work with are so important. If they don't know what they are doing, it can be extremely dangerous for everyone involved.

SPIRIT PHOTOGRAPHY

Just as spirits can let us know they're around in photographs, we can deliberately set out to take pictures of ghosts. Often during my workshops participants take pictures of me while I am onstage. Hundreds, even thousands, of orbs appear in their photos. Are they ghosts? Yes, I believe ghostly energy has been captured.

Cameras are a must on any ghost-hunting expedition. Many ghost enthusiasts have successfully captured ghostly images on film. However, you do not have to be part of a ghost-hunting group for ghostly images to appear in your photographs. When working with spirit photography, the key component is your intuition. You may have an urge to take a picture at a particular moment or to aim the camera at a certain angle. Listen with your inner voice; let your instinct be your guide. When attempting to capture ghosts on film, I recommend the following:

- Designate a photographer. Only one person should take the picture. There may be several others present to help feed energy, but use only one photographer, and that person should be the same throughout the event.

- Never call out to a spirit to reveal itself. You never know what may show up. Take the photo only when you instinctively feel it is time to do so or when you are instructed by a ghost.

- Bring more than one camera and lots of film and batteries. Save all the negatives, or camera cards, because many times an image will form after your first look.

Let me add something that I have noticed about holding on to spirit photos. The best way to store these special photos is in a covered dark place, like a box or a book, because often such photos seem to keep developing on their own. Sometimes after several months, or even years, have gone by, a photo looks different from when first taken. You may notice light or orbs around something that was not there when the picture was first taken. This is exactly what happened with the spirit photo of my brother-in-law Dennis. At first, my sister could see only his profile, but a month later, when I saw the picture, we could see him quite clearly, as well as two other spirits in the background. One of the spirits looked like my mother.

Again, let me say that the best place to capture ghosts, lights, and orbs on film is in a place where there are people. Don't go to a cemetery or empty lot. Ghosts are always around live, vibrant energy, especially the energy of their loved ones.

THE CAT LADY

I was doing a guest appearance on a TV show when Evan, one of the crew members, came up to me, all out of breath. He started to ask me a lot of questions about ghosts.

"How do you get rid of ghosts in your house?"

I suggested that he explain the situation to me.

"A couple of friends of mine just moved into a 1930s bungalow in Hollywood, and there's all sorts of weird stuff going on."

"Like what?"

"Loud noises. Doors crashing shut. Creaking sounds."

"Anything else?"

"They told me they have had plumbing problems. Their water pipes have burst, and the house was just inspected before they moved in. I myself have felt cold breezes in parts of the house. They knew you would be on the show and asked me to ask you for help."

"It sounds to me like it's an earthbound ghost, and I specialize in those that have crossed into the light."

Evan looked dejected. I continued, "But I will go with you and try to see what the disturbance is and help the spirit move on."

Evan's face lit up. "Great! I'll tell my friends. They'll be so relieved."

Wally and Lisa Mackel ushered me into their living room at six o'clock the following evening. When I arrived, I was also introduced to Marlene, Bert, and Rob, a local ghost-busting team.

I asked Lisa, "Why do you want me here when you have a ghost-hunting team already?"

Lisa responded, "I thought it wouldn't hurt to have strength in numbers so we can catch the ghost."

I laughed. "One thing has nothing to do with the other. I usually work by myself."

I didn't think that Marlene, who was obviously the ghost-busting team leader, appreciated my comment.

"I will do whatever you want, but I have to ask that you all stay out of the room when I am working." I didn't want their excitement or fear to interfere with my efforts.

The members of the team shrugged and moved into another area of the house.

I explained about the ghost world and how I worked. "I can sense when the energy in a place is being disturbed. I can't make any promises, but I will do whatever I can do to help bring peace to your home."

As I sat with Lisa and Wally, a spirit came into focus and stood next to Lisa.

"There is a person by the name of Ralph here." I looked at Lisa. "He is in the light and is tied to you."

Lisa acknowledged Ralph. "Yes, he is my father, who has passed. I have called upon him many times to protect me and Wally from any evil in the house."

At that exact moment, Marlene and her team tramped through the living room. Marlene called out in a loud voice, "I'm not picking up any ghost energy by her."

"That's because you're not a medium," I answered.

"Whatever!" Marlene mumbled something derogatory about mediums and crystal balls.

"Ralph is telling me that there are two people, a man and a woman, who are causing the problems." As soon as he said this, Ralph then left rapidly, and we were left with even more questions.

Then I began to do my ritual for clearing a house. I walked through each room and registered the impressions I received. I could tell right away where there was an imbalance in the energy or whether there was a malevolent spirit around. I could also pick up the emotional nature of the ghost. I started in the master bedroom, where everything seemed to be fine. Then I walked into the back pantry, where I immediately picked up the energy of an older woman who was quite upset about something.

"It seems like she hangs out right here, going back and forth."

"Yes!" Lisa said. "The cupboards open and close every day at the same time. Right here!"

"Wow!" screamed Marlene. "How cool. Look, Lisa."

Marlene not only interrupted my investigation but was interfering with the energy of the room. Marlene did not have good energy. She showed Lisa and Wally an orb that Rob caught on the camera.

I walked into the living room, and once again I saw Ralph.

Who is stuck in the house? I asked him.

He explained to me, *There's a woman here from the twenties. She is very angry because she used to have seventeen cats, and she can't find any of them. She thinks someone took them from her, and she won't leave until she finds them.*

I thought to myself, *She will never leave here.*

Ralph continued. *Her husband passed into the light and comes around to try to bring her over, but she doesn't see him because she is so obsessed over those cats.*

When Wally and Lisa entered, I told them what Ralph said.

"Amazing," said Wally. "We'll have to check who the former owners were."

Marlene came by again, and I noticed there was something stuck to her. It seemed to be a low-level entity. I didn't dare say anything.

When she walked by me, she said, "Cats? You are so wrong." Marlene and her "ghost-busting team" left the house, completely unaware that there was negative energy attached to her and one of her cameramen. Some ghost-busters.

Very shortly after they left, the real fun began. Wally, Lisa, and I were sitting on their couch as I explained the difference between earthbound ghosts and those who have passed into the light. Suddenly two cupboard doors opened in the pantry with a smacking sound! We rushed there to look. Immediately, we all smelled the lovely scent of gardenias. Then I felt something cross in front of me.

"Ahhh!" Lisa screamed. She looked at me and said, "I felt someone walk right through me."

As I was about to assist her, the front door whooshed opened and banged against the wall. That startled everyone. As I looked toward the front door, I saw a young-looking gentleman, dressed in a tuxedo, holding out his hand. It dawned on me that this was the old lady's husband coming to bring her over.

I quickly sent a thought to the earthbound ghost. *It is time for you to follow your husband home. He is here to rescue you. All your cats are with him.*

Unfortunately, I did not receive any communication back from her, so I didn't know if my words had any effect.

As I kept my eyes on the husband, several different cats ran into the room and surrounded his feet. It was very odd. It felt like feeding time in a shelter. I kept sending the thought over and over to the old lady. I thought by then she must have seen her cats.

Then the husband smiled as he held out his hand once again. I knew at last that he was greeting his wife.

I turned to Wally and Lisa, but they seemed to know what I was about to say.

"She's gone, isn't she?" asked Lisa.

"I believe so," I responded.

"You can tell. It seems so much lighter in here."

I replied, "It's because she is where she should be."

The young couple were so appreciative and kept thanking me.

"Keep the wonderful energy you have created together alive and joyful in this house. Keep spreading the word about life after death."

As they ushered me out the front door, Lisa turned on the porch light. I looked down and gasped. There on the second step was a small brown bird; its neck was broken.

"Perhaps one of the cats left it here as a token of its love."

ELECTRONIC VOICE PHENOMENON

On occasion, a ghost can materialize the sound of its physical voice on electromagnetic tape, an occurrence called an Electronic Voice Phenomenon (EVP). Ghost hunters have successfully captured actual voices of spirits with the use of tape recorders. When using this method, the investigator should place the recorder in a "hot area"—a place where a majority of ghostly activity occurs. When the actual tape is running, you will not hear anything. However, when the tape is played back, usually at slower speeds, brief words or phrases spoken by a ghost may be detected. It seems that most of the messages are benign or jibberish, but occasionally words are completely understandable.

Electronic Voice Phenomena have been acquired on all types of electronics, from cheap tape recorders and ham radios to televisions and computers. I have had the wonderful pleasure of speaking to the founder of the American Association of Electronic Voice Phenomena (AAEVP), Sarah Esteph, who has chronicled hundreds of hours of spirit voices and whispers. She runs an incredible organization that is known around the globe, and her integrity and honesty with the work is supreme.

If EVP interests you, be aware that any time you delve into the unseen world, you may get more than you bargain for. The messages that come through can be frivolous or downright scary.

I will never forget the e-mail—and eventually a tape—I received in 1997 from an extremely upset young woman visiting my Web site to contact me for advice. Becky, who unfortunately didn't know anything about EVP, was a musician and quasi-sound engineer who worked in a makeshift studio at her house in Santa Barbara, California. Several times a week, local bands would come into her studio and record. Late one night Becky was working on some tracks that had been laid down that afternoon. In the middle of the second song, she very distinctly heard a man's voice quickly say, "Your father's gonna die!" Becky played the track over and over. The words were on a very low tone level on the soundboard. She thought maybe one of the band members was playing a joke on her. So the next day, when the band came into the studio, she had them all listen to the playback. All of them were flabbergasted.

Becky told me, "My father and I had a falling-out, and we haven't spoken in four years."

"That's interesting," I said.

"Several months ago, I kept thinking of him. I wondered if I should buy a plane ticket and go back home to Iowa and visit so I could square things up with him."

"Did you?"

"Work took all my time and energy. I never did get around to going back home."

"Is the voice on the tape familiar?"

"No. I can't identify it."

Two days after our web chat, Becky got a phone call from her sister in Iowa. Her father had died.

It was obvious to me that a ghost had been trying to warn her.

OUIJA BOARD

The Ouija Board—or "talking board," as it was originally called—is probably the most misunderstood divining tool in history. The original boards were first seen in the mid-1800s during the rise of Spiritualism. In those days, the talking board consisted of a large, dining room-size table with letters around the outer edge. A triangular-shaped indicator, or "planchette," was used to point to the letters. People would place their fingers on the planchette and ask a question. The planchette would move from letter to letter, spelling out messages from the spirit world. Though the design and look have changed dramatically over the past one hundred years, the board is still used in the same way to contact the world of ghosts.

In 1966 Parker Brothers marketed the "Ouija Board" as a family game geared toward children. The company never really acknowledged its validity as a divination tool. As the Ouija Board's popularity grew, many soon realized that it was hardly a children's game. I believe that the Ouija Board has been the subject of many false tales of demonic possession, entity influence, and even schizophrenia owing to ignorance, misinformation, and various religious belief systems.

In truth, the Ouija Board can be used to help a person open up to his or her intuitive self. The principle is similar to using a crystal ball, pendulum, divining rod, tarot cards, runes, or several other tools designed for gaining insight. Using a Ouija Board for the right reason and in the correct way, a person can increase his or her sensitivity and gain spiritual insights. Used incorrectly, however, it can become a Pandora's box, opening the user up to lower, unevolved entities and negative energy. Before delving into any type of metaphysical work, you need to have gained a full understanding of the instrument involved and a proper respect for what you are asking it to do. An ample amount of protection is also essential.

I first started using the Ouija Board over twenty years ago, and I have never had any problems with ghostly attachments or possessions or anything of a negative nature. In fact, I am sure a lot of you will be shocked to learn that I developed some of my mediumship skills of discernment by working with the Ouija Board.

Shortly after moving to Los Angeles from New York, I met my good friend and fellow intuitive Carol Shoemaker. We were at her house one evening when she said to me, "Do you want to do the board?"

I looked at Carol with a blank stare. I didn't have the slightest idea what she was talking about. "What board? The only board I know is the ironing board!"

"No, silly, the Ouija Board. I used to use it every weekend with my Aunt Vinnie so we could find out what was going to happen in the upcoming months. It was like listening to a weather forecast."

At first, I was skeptical, but I knew Carol was a good person and not a nut, so I agreed. Carol gave me a quick tutorial in doing the board:

- Purify the space by lighting incense to keep unwanted and lower energies, or stragglers, as she called them, far away from the area.

- Put out a bowl of water, which acts as a conductor of energy to spirits and helps them transmit messages. (A side note: Have you ever noticed how often you receive insightful information in the shower or bathtub? Water is a great conductor of energy.)

- Light a candle to draw a light of protection around everyone participating.

- Play pleasant music in the background. Light music can also raise the vibration to a very high level.

- The next and most important part of the ritual is to take several minutes to meditate and center yourselves.

Carol told me to focus on love and to visualize a white light all around us. We did this for about ten minutes.

Having grown up Catholic, I was very comfortable with the formality of a ritual, and I realized that this one had all the elements of a Catholic Mass. I began to feel wonderful and light. When we opened our eyes, we placed our fingers on the planchette. Carol explained that the spirit people would meld themselves into our auras and impress us to move the indicator from letter to letter.

"You will probably feel their emotional state and their personality," she said.

Well, I was ready. Immediately, I felt an incredible tingling sensation in my hands. I looked at Carol.

She asked, "Do you feel that?"

"Ah, yes, it feels like pins and needles."

Suddenly the planchette began to make circles at a record speed. It was almost impossible to hold on.

I looked over at Carol in amazement. "Are you doing that?"

"No, James, that is spirit. They do that to bring up the energy before they can speak."

I felt a surge of delightful electricity run through me. I also felt an amazing amount of love.

Carol and I looked at the board as it began to spell out words.

JAMES I AM ANGEL LOVE. I AM YOUR SOUL GUIDE. I WILL WORK WITH YOU IN BRINGING OTHER SOULS TO THE LIGHT OF UNDER-STANDING AND TRUTH.

I felt like I had had amnesia and this was a remembrance from my spiritual life. It felt so real and right.

The session continued for a few more hours. Other souls, like Carol's father, her Aunt Vinnie, and my grandmother, showed up and gave us a "weather forecast" for our futures. Many of the prophecies have come to pass.

I thanked Carol. I felt as though I had discovered a whole new part of my being. We did the board a few times a month for many years, and it certainly aided in my spiritual development.

A few days after that first session I was checking out a New Age bookstore. When I turned to the sale table next to the register, I spotted a cassette tape of spiritual music entitled *Angel Love*. So I bought it.

DREAMS

Whenever I do a workshop, one of the first questions I ask the audience is, "How many of you have had dreams of a loved one who has passed over?" A good 90 percent of them usually raise their hands. They all agree that when they have a dream of their loved one, it feels extremely real and seems to be much more than a dream. Some admit that they don't even want to return to the waking state. This is very understandable. I do believe the experience feels so real because at night when we sleep our spirit bodies leave our physical bodies and go to the other side. We visit our loved ones, guides, pets, and soul mates from ages past.

You know the expression "If you have a problem, sleep on it." I believe that you can evaluate any problem better when you are out of conscious reality, where you can understand the full nature of the experience from the spiritual side of life.

If you want to contact family members in a very safe and easy way, ask your loved ones to appear in your dreams just before going to sleep. In a few days, or maybe a week, you will see them. I recommend that you also keep a dream journal next to your bed so that you can quickly write down your experience in the dream state. The more time that passes after the dream, the more likely you will start forgetting it.

If you want to know your spirit guide, ask him or her to appear in your dreams and tell you what type of guide he or she is and what his or her work entails. Believe me, it works.

I incorporate a technique on one of my meditation CDs that helps students get to know their guides. I cannot tell you how many e-mails people send me to say that, not only were they able to see their guides, but sometimes they were surprised at who showed up.

One lady felt somewhat exasperated by the exercise. She said that she played the CD every night before going to bed, and every morning she would wake up dreaming about her dead dog.

She was shocked when I told her, "Your dog is probably one of your guides."

"For what?" she asked. "How can a dog be a guide?"

"Well, think about it," I replied. "One of the most endearing characteristics of a dog is protection. Your dog is protecting you from the other side."

When the woman realized that her beloved pet was still watching over her, she felt a sense of relief to know that she was never alone.

MEDIUMSHIP

A medium is an individual who is able to contact the spirit world through psychic phenomena that are either physical or mental in nature. As a mental medium, I have various abilities to communicate with the world beyond, including:

- *Clairvoyance*: Commonly known as "second sight," clairvoyance is the means by which a medium can visually see ghosts, pictures, symbols, or images in his or her mind's eye.

- *Clairaudience*: Using this form of mediumship, a medium can hear spirit voices as sounds or read a spirit's thoughts that come into his or her mind.

- *Clairsentience*: This is the most common form of mental mediumship. A medium can sense and feel a spirit's energy as well as its emotional state and personality.

The other type of mediumship is physical. A medium with this ability is harder to find nowadays. It is a phenomenal gift with the following attributes:

- *Transfiguration*: A spirit superimposes its face on the medium's face, and those in the room can see the visible characteristics of a deceased person's face.

- *Apports*: Completely solid objects can materialize out of thin air through a physical medium. Often ghosts will make coins, flowers, keys, or stones appear.

- *Automatic writing*: A physical medium can write messages under the influence of a ghost. Depending on the amount of blending of ghost with medium, many times the ghost's own penmanship style will appear.

- *Trance or trance channel*: The medium falls into a trance, allowing a spirit to take control of his or her body. There are many degrees of trance, from deep to light. Deep trance is the optimal way for a spirit to come through completely.

- *Materialization*: Under the right conditions, a spirit draws an ethereal substance known as ectoplasm out of the medium, and others around him, and manipulates this ectoplasm so that the spirit takes on physical form.

- *Direct voice*: Here again, a spirit draws out ectoplasm from a medium and creates an artificial voice box. The spirit concentrates its energies through this voice box and speaks in an earthly voice.

THE PHYSICAL MEDIUM LESLIE FLYNT

When I was developing my mediumship abilities, I had the wonderful experience of sitting with a very kind soul. Brian E. Hurst was the first one to discover my abilities. Every summer Brian would host Leslie Flynt, the physical medium I spoke about earlier in the book. Leslie was in his late seventies and would rarely sit for people, but when he traveled to the United States, he would do an evening séance for Brian and several other guests. I was fortunate enough to be invited to several of those incredible evenings. I attended four such sittings, and each time I was filled with a heightened sense of anticipation and uncertainty. It certainly took courage to sit in the dark and listen to otherworldly voices, wondering what they would say.

It was about seven in the evening, and ten of us were squeezed together in the small back bedroom of Brian's modest bungalow on Irving Place in Hollywood. Because Leslie was a physical "direct voice" medium, the room had to be completely void of light in order for the ectoplasm to manifest. I remember sitting on one of the couches with a man to my right and a woman on my left. It was the middle of the summer, so the heat of the day was still holding tight in the room.

Brian turned off all the lights, and I was immediately transported back to my childhood when we would sit in a tent in our basement and exchange ghost stories, each one scarier than the last. As an adult, I found it somehow even stranger to be sitting in total darkness waiting for ghosts. This was the real thing, and it was extremely uncomfortable. All I could hear was the sound of people breathing, waiting for a ghost to make contact. We made small talk for the next twenty minutes as the ectoplasm slowly and delicately emerged from Leslie's nose and mouth, creating an artificial larynx. Suddenly I felt an extreme chill around my neck, and it moved down my leg. I shivered, not from the unexpected cold, but more for what it represented. Other people felt it too.

Someone said, "Did you feel that chill?"

Another person uttered, "Did you hear that?"

I quickly moved my head from one side to the other.

"Has anyone seen a ghost?" I asked.

"No, not yet," several people responded in chorus.

All of a sudden a high-pitched piercing sound ripped through the air, causing some of us to jump off the couch in fright. Then a voice screamed out to us in the dark.

Can you hear me now? It was the distinct cockney accent of Mickey, Leslie's spirit guide. Mickey was a newspaper boy in the early 1900s. He was hit by a horse and buggy and died. Mickey was Leslie's control who organized the ghosts who were going to speak to us.

From the center of the ceiling, I could hear Mickey's voice. *Hey, is that you, Ursula? You're a funny one, you are!*

"Thank you, Mickey. I'm so glad that I amuse you," Ursula responded.

What? he shouted back.

"I am happy you find me amusing," she repeated.

Oh, I find you amusing all right! Ha!

Mickey was extremely loud. We were in such a small room that his voice seemed to bellow like a circus barker.

Leslie remarked, "Mickey seems to have quite a bit of energy this particular evening."

Meanwhile, I was in awe of the whole situation. I was definitely on a wild ride into the unknown, and the experience was one of those rare ones that happen only once in a lifetime.

Mickey made a personal comment to each person in the room. When he came to me, he exclaimed, *Yes, you are James. Has anyone ever told you that you're a psychic?*

"Yes, they have, Mickey," I nervously shouted back.

Without missing a beat, he shrieked, *Well, then, what are you doing about it?*

"I am sitting in a development circle," I responded, and he was off.

It was such a startling experience that I had to take a moment to gather in what had just happened. When I realized that the spirit voice was real, I started to shake and perspire.

Mickey brought through several other speakers who wanted to connect with someone in the crowd. I sat there hoping that someone I knew would come through and I could prove once and for all that what I was hearing was real.

Then it happened. A French male voice called, *Can you hear me? Can you hear me? I want to speak to James. I want to speak to James.*

I almost fell over. *Who in the world was this French man, and what was he going to say to me?*

James, you are a sensitive, a psychic, a creative person. You know, when I was in your world, I too was a creative person. I was an artist. James, we are working with you. We have many big plans for you, my friend. What I say now you will not understand, but in time you will. We are looking to you, my friend. Can you hear me? One day you will write a book and help many people. You will travel over water to help many people. Do you understand me?

I was so nervous. I could remember thinking, *I hope someone is taping all of this.* Thankfully, someone was.

Then I asked, "Is my mother around?"

The Frenchman said, *Wait.*

Then Mickey interrupted. *Did your mother have a chest condition?*
"Yes, Mickey, she did. Is she there?"
She's here all right. Hold on, he responded.

The moment I was waiting for finally arrived. I heard my mother's voice. *Jamie . . . Jamie, can you hear me?*

I began to cry. I had not heard her voice since she died three years earlier.

"Yes, I can, Mom."

She continued, *I love you. I love you. I love you.*

Then the energy started to fail, and she was gone.

That evening was one of the most fortunate experiences I have ever had. I will never forget it, and I have a tape to relive every moment of it. The amazing thing is that the Frenchman's information made no sense to me in 1987, but it certainly did after my first book, *Talking to Heaven*, was published in 1997. I had to travel over water to promote the book.

It just goes to show you that you never know who is nearby, but I assure you that some ghost is always looking after you.

TEN

Protection

When people learn that I can talk to the dead, the first thing they ask is, "Is anybody around me now?" The next thing I notice is that undeniable "deer caught in the headlights" look. Eyes widen with fright as they fire the second question at me. "Doesn't it scare you?" It seems that the living, although curious, are also extremely squeamish about being surrounded by an invisible world of beings.

Why are people so scared? Could it be that all those horror movies have tainted our belief systems and reference points? Or is it because we have always been afraid of death and dying?

Should we be afraid of ghosts? What exactly are we supposed to protect ourselves from? Knowledge is power, and if we know more about ghosts, we won't feel afraid when we feel them among us.

Throughout the book, I have stated that everything is energy, including your thoughts. Merely by thinking about someone, you are focusing and sending energy directly to that person. These living thought forms cannot be detected by your five senses. If someone sends you negative emotional thoughts, such as *I hate you* or *You're a loser and won't amount to anything*, you may feel the effect of such thoughts without realizing the source. Negative thoughts can enter your field of energy, or aura, and if you have not properly protected yourself, the negative thought forms can gradually build up in your mind and body. The results can be detrimental to your well-being and peace of mind. You are under what is referred to as "psychic attack."

How do you know if you are under psychic attack? Usually it takes a while for the negative energy to build up, but when it does, it can be diagnosed by the following symptoms: you are easily irritated; you are experiencing bouts of insomnia, depression, or unfounded anger; you feel overly exhausted; and you have continuous thoughts of fear and loss of control. There is a sense that you are "not yourself," and truthfully, you are not. You are being influenced by the negative energy that has penetrated your aura. This energy has seeped into all areas of your being and clouded your judgment. Psychic attack affects every dimension of your life—the emotional, physical, mental, and spiritual.

During my show *Beyond* the schedule was grueling. We taped four shows a day, two in the morning, and two in the afternoon. Each show included two individual readings for people picked in advance by the production staff. To keep the integrity of the show intact, I was not involved in the selection of these people. My office was separated from the rest of the production staff, and I was not in touch with the producers until the day of the taping. Looking back, I wish I had had more of a hand in how the producers picked people and situations, because the readings were unusually emotional in nature and ranged anywhere from the murder of an entire wedding party to a mother who smothered her children to death. Needless to say, I was thrown into all sorts of disturbing situations, and I felt much like a Christian being thrown into the lions' den. It was very difficult for me to be a part of a show involving spirit communication while those producing the show had no clue about the sensitive nature of a medium or the damaging effects of other people's unstable emotional energy.

Unfortunately, the nature of television is sensationalistic, and the producers have all the control. Since the executive producer of *Beyond* could not predict the outcome of my readings, she instructed the segment producers (unbeknownst to me) to find people in severely desperate situations. She assumed that the more emotional and layered an event, the better chance I would have of getting clear and accurate communication. The layers may not have come through, but exceptionally real human drama did.

Even with years of experience, I could not predict the toll these negative and distressing situations would take on me. Because I had to open myself up to the spirit world, I would invite all sorts of energy into my aura. I was constantly centering and grounding myself through meditation and visualization techniques, but exposure to such negative energy still left me vulnerable to horrendous emotional upheaval. No matter how much protection I surrounded myself with, the constant barrage of negative, hurtful, and painful energy took its toll on my psyche. It was as if I were a target on a firing range wearing only a bulletproof vest.

After several months of communicating with homicides, suicides, and other forms of human depravity and destruction, I was unable to get a good night's sleep. My diet was off; I ate stuff I had never eaten before. I became irritated at the drop of a hat. It never occurred to me that my worn-out feelings were due to the readings. I assumed I was exhausted from long hours of taping and a very hectic schedule. However, it was much more than that.

Eventually, I made an appointment with my good friend Michael Tamura, a renowned psychic healer. Michael is very gifted, not only at pulling out energy on a psychic level but at discerning its characteristics and its source. During the two-hour session, Michael peeled off several layers of energy belonging to many dead people. What surprised me, however, was the amount of energy he pulled off from the people in the audience who had bizarre expectations of what I would reveal. The most interesting energy that Michael peeled off my aura was the fearful energy of network executives and the show's producers. Michael explained that one of the female producers was invalidated as a child and she "needed" the television series to become a hit so that she could feel as successful as her male counterparts.

To say the least, I was amazed at Michael's findings. After his healing intervention, I felt like my old self again. Surges of incredible energy ran through my body. That night I had the first good night's sleep I'd had in months, and I was less irritable and impatient than I had been. (I will describe Michael's protection technique later in this chapter.)

Michael reminded me of something I had known but forgot to use on my own behalf. When we give our energy to others, we have to get it back; otherwise, we eventually feel depleted. Ever since that time, whenever I read for someone, the same evening I meditate on the person and visualize my own energy leaving him or her and returning to me. It works! Never again have I felt that enormous sense of exhaustion and irritation.

GHOSTS ON THE PROWL

I believe that a ghost can invade a person's aura and influence the physical vessel in order to relive a particular physical experience. In the previous chapter, I explained how a ghost can have a harmful influence on the living when I discussed possession. When a ghost invades your space, you can suffer from frequent headaches, unusual body aches, indigestion and stomach prob-

lems, earaches, sore throats, and depression. You may have atypical thoughts and behaviors or dreams and nightmares that are
particularly abnormal.

There are many key signs that can alert you that a ghost is in-
habiting your physical space:

- The ambience in the room seems dark or dense. Whenever
  I go to a place where there is a lot of ghostly activity, the
  room feels a bit heavy, as if I am walking through tar.

- There are unexplainable electrical surges in your house or
  in machinery and appliances like lights, computers, televisions, radios, garage doors, and Jacuzzis. If your appliances
  turn on and off by themselves, you can bet you're sharing
  space with an earthbound entity.

- There is a distinct smell in the room or the scent of a perfume that is unrecognizable.

- Temperature changes are also a telltale sign. You feel cold
  spots in one particular area of your house. Perhaps you feel
  cold breezes around you or goose bumps and chills. Cold
  spots and breezes when windows and doors are closed or
  the heat is on is a sure sign that a ghost is draining energy
  in those areas.

- You feel that someone is watching you when there is no one
  around.

- You feel as if someone has touched you.

- You hear a knocking or rapping sound, footsteps, banging,
  voices, whispers, or music.

- Out of the corner of your eye, you see a small flickering of
  lights. These are known as spirit lights.

- Objects in your home have been moved from one place to another without your touching them. Or objects completely disappear and you never find them again.

- The water in your house turns on and off of its own accord.

- Your pet's behavior seems strange. You see your cat or dog staring at something in the air that is not there.

- You notice impressions or indentations on the bed, couch, or chairs that were not there before.

- The telephone rings and no one is on the other end. Instead, you hear a lot of static.

- You have thoughts that are not your own, as happened with my nonsmoking friend who felt the urge to buy cigarettes.

THE ANGRY GHOST

The term *poltergeist* comes from the German and means "noisy spirit." It first made its way into the mainstream vernacular with the popularity of the 1980s Steven Spielberg movie *Poltergeist*. The types of activity associated with poltergeists include strange noises, moving or disappearing objects, and unpleasant odors. Perhaps owing in part to how these spirits are depicted in movies, many people believe that poltergeist activity has to do with an angry ghost, or one that wants a lot of attention. I believe that a poltergeist is not necessarily an evil ghost, but perhaps one that can gather up enough energy in the environment to manifest in a strong and obvious way.

Poltergeist activity usually occurs very abruptly and ends just as abruptly. So far no one knows why. Even paranormal scientists who study such activity debate the origin of the activity and the origin of a poltergeist itself. Many believe that a majority of the cases revolve around what is known as an "agent." An agent is a living person, usually a woman or child, who seems to display an enormous amount of the phenomenon known as psychokinesis, which is caused by the person's subconscious mind. In other words, someone's mind is active enough to make objects hurl around the room. It is quite rare. However, I believe that the mind is capable of anything.

Several years ago, I was at my local health food store, wandering the aisles, looking for toothpaste. Suddenly I felt a tap on my shoulder. I turned to look, and a rather tall, lean man, with brown hair, in his late twenties, stood in front of me. He seemed extremely nervous.

The young man stuttered, "Ahh . . . please forgive me, ahh . . . but are you Mr. Praagh?"

"Van Praagh," I corrected him.

"Please forgive me for bothering you, but I recognized you from television and thought you might be able to help me."

"I no longer do private readings," I told him.

"I . . . I don't really want a reading. At least I don't think I do, but I don't know where else to turn."

I could detect the desperate tone in his voice.

"Take a breath," I said. Then I suggested that we go to the side of the store where there were tables and chairs so that we could sit down and talk.

As the two of us walked toward the seating area, the young man kept thanking me for taking the time to speak with him.

Once we sat down, the young man said, "I'm Mike, by the way. I came here to find some candles or incense that could take away evil spirits."

"Why do you think there are evil spirits around you?"

"Because my wife and I have been bothered by lots of weird things in the house, like objects moving, terrible smells. We even heard voices. What else could it be?"

"Let's start from the beginning. Tell me exactly what is happening."

"My wife, Hanna, and I moved to Long Beach two years ago. I inherited the house from my father after a long and intense legal battle. Finally, I was given the house."

"What was your relationship with your father like before he passed?" I asked.

"Fine," Mike answered. "My father and I always got along."

"Then why was there a problem getting the house?"

"It was my stepmother. She wanted to have all of my father's money and possessions, but she wasn't entitled to it all. She sued me for the house."

"Are you cordial with her now?" I continued.

"No. We don't talk at all. Especially not after what she did to my dad. We think she tried to poison him."

"Really?" I said in astonishment. "How do you know?"

Mike explained. "When we went for a visit, I found some lethal substances in the kitchen pantry."

I was a bit surprised and asked Mike to continue to tell me about the house he inherited.

"Ever since my wife went into her sixth month of pregnancy, neither of us has slept through the night. There is so much noise in the house that it keeps us awake." The young man began crying. "This is our first baby, and we are concerned that whatever this thing is, it's after our baby." He looked at me with tearful eyes. "What am I gonna do?"

I felt a stabbing in my heart at the thought of something trying to attack a baby, but I did my best to calm Mike down.

"Can you be more specific about the noises and racket in the house?"

"Every night, actually around one in the morning, the lights in the hallway flicker. We hear a mumbled crying sound and a banging in the back bedroom. It's the room we are planning to use for the baby. It goes on for about fifteen minutes. I get up each time and walk into the bedroom. It always feels weird, like someone is watching me. I get goose bumps every time."

"How long has this been going on?"

"Five weeks. I even called the local Catholic church, but the priests were not really interested in what I had to say."

Mike hesitated. "Do you think it might be my father? Maybe he's unhappy about the plans we made to change the house."

"That's possible," I said, "but I doubt he would cause that kind of disturbance. The only way to find out is for me to go and see for myself."

I took down Mike's phone number, and a few days later I called him to schedule a visit to his house near Belmont Shore in Long Beach.

A week later, at six in the evening, I arrived at Mike and Hanna's house. I would have preferred to meet at one o'clock in the morning, when the disturbances actually occurred, but because that would have been so late, we settled on a more reasonable time. Hanna, who was very pregnant, welcomed me inside.

"I've been having the weirdest dreams," she said. "One in particular I've been having quite a lot. I keep seeing a tree house fall out of a tree and crash to the ground."

"Is it all right if I walk around and see if I can pick up anything?" I asked.

"Of course," she smiled.

As I roamed from room to room, I didn't feel anything especially unusual or sinister. The energy felt as normal as it does in any other house. However, when I reached the back bedroom, I noticed a cold breeze as I entered the room. I felt as if the room didn't belong to the rest of the house. Suddenly I became very anxious and could not wait to get out of there. I returned to the living room and sat down. I stared at Mike, hoping that his deceased father would appear and we would find out the reason for the disturbances, but his father never showed up.

I looked at Hanna and didn't get much from her, except for a name.

"Does the name Annabelle mean anything to you?"

"No," she replied.

Then I got a hit on only one other thing. "Does canning tomatoes ring a bell?"

"All I know," Hanna said, "was that my grandmother lived on a farm in Iowa, and I used to hear stories about her canning all types of things. Tomatoes were her specialty."

It seemed so far-fetched, but that was all I could get. I did not feel that the noises were associated with the grandmother at all.

"I want you both to keep a journal and to make it as specific as possible, accounting for everything that happens."

Then I helped them to psychically clean out their house, although in all sincerity, I did not feel any bad energy except in that one bedroom. I thought it couldn't hurt, and psychologically, clearing the house might ease their fears.

About four months later, Mike called. "It's a boy. We named him Walter after my dad."

Mike talked about the baby, but I could tell something wasn't right.

"Any more problems in the house?"

Mike hesitated. "No, well, not really. To tell you the truth, we are counting our blessings."

"What do you mean?"

"Well, when we brought Walter home, the noises started again and got worse. The furniture in the baby's room would move around in really weird formations. At one point we thought we heard a voice call out 'Anna.' Hanna and I were scared, and we decided to keep Walter with us in our room. Three days after we brought Walter home, there was a terrible thunderstorm, and the wind rattled the house. At one o'clock in the morning, we heard this terrible crashing sound. Hanna and I ran into Walter's room and were stunned at what we saw. A tree had fallen through the roof right onto Walter's crib. If Walter had been there, he would have been crushed to death."

Needless to say, Mike's story came as a complete shock to me. It was like hearing something on the nightly news.

Mike continued. "This is where it gets even freakier."

I remember sitting down to listen to the rest of what he had to say.

"You know the message you gave us about Hanna's grand-mother?"

"Yes. About canning tomatoes. I remember."

"Hanna asked her mother about the name Annabelle. Her mother told her that Annabelle was the name of her older sister who had died of crib death. Hanna's grandmother blamed herself for the baby's death and was never able to forgive herself for it. We think it must have been Hanna's grandmother making sure Walter was protected. She was trying to warn us with the noises and the nightmares."

"No, I don't think it was Hanna's grandmother. I think it was the baby, Annabelle herself, who wanted to protect little Walter."

"Come to think of it," Mike replied, "last night Hanna had a dream of a little girl playing in a tree house, and she said the girl was all smiles."

This ghost story ends on a positive note because little Annabelle was motivated to protect the new baby. However, I have had hundreds of letters from people who have had very different and rather unhappy outcomes with poltergeists that slam doors, move furniture, and screech and holler. It takes an enormous amount of energy for earthbound ghosts to manifest in such chilling ways. If this kind of phenomenon occurs in your home, I would suggest that you see a well-respected person in the paranormal field who deals with the grounding and centering of energy.

However, before you decide that a poltergeist is around, make sure that the activity is not originating from a person with a lot of psychokinetic energy. If this type of activity does originate from a living person rather than a ghost, the person needs to learn techniques to control the outbursts and direct the energy in a positive way. The best advice I can give is to make sure you protect yourself. Remember that negative energy can enter only if you are depleted of your own energy. Prayer and meditation are the best ways to build up your energy field. You don't have to be afraid; you just have to be aware. The following pages contain exercises that you can do to shield your aura from negative energy.

WHAT IS THE AURA?

First of all, I want to explain just what the aura is. The *aura,* or what I like to call our "sacred space," is the electromagnetic energy field that surrounds and encompasses the atmosphere of every living thing. The "auric shell" comprises various layers, each one distinct but interconnected within the shell. The aura has often been referred to as a "halo" and is depicted in religious paintings, especially those of Jesus, saints, and angels.

The aura encompasses the essence of the living being it surrounds, and it projects the thoughts, desires, and mental, emotional, physical, and spiritual states of the individual. A person's innate spiritual gifts are clearly defined in the aura, and I have had the privilege of seeing many individuals' talents and aptitudes when I look at their auras.

For instance, at a recent workshop I saw brightly colored musical notes above a lady's head. I asked her if she was involved with music, and she replied, "Yes. I've always had a knack for music, but I never really pursued it professionally."

When I hear that a person has a knack for something but doesn't do anything about it, I feel that the person is not in touch with who he or she is. If this woman had used her natural musical abilities, she would have been extremely successful in the musical field. However, fear, life circumstances, family situations, or other reasons may have caused her not to follow her calling, and she did not use her talents in this lifetime. She won't necessarily lose her talents, but they will not expand if they are not used.

Not only is the aura an energy that envelops you, but it penetrates your being as well. The aura is a colorful field of energy, and its colors represent your level of vitality, mental capacity, emotional well-being, and spiritual understanding. The dominant color represents the dominant part of your makeup. If you are very spiritual and compassionate, you will tend to have more green and purple in your aura.

We are all protected naturally by our auric shell, but at times this shell can wear down if not properly protected. Cracks and holes can appear in it. All sorts of psychic energy, ghostly or otherwise, can enter through these cracks and holes. Anyone can overdo something and not be aware of losing energy. I certainly didn't realize that my auric field was so depleted while doing my TV series.

A weakened and unhealthy aura can also be the result of drug overuse, alcohol abuse, constant negative thoughts and beliefs, and fearful and angry emotions. Also, if you are around negative locations and negative people, you are susceptible to losing energy. Finally, a variety of illnesses and diseases can deplete the aura.

It is important to remember that our thoughts and emotions affect our auras first and manifest lastly in our physical bodies. We should be mindful on a daily basis of reinforcing the strength of our auras through prayer, meditation, and positive visualization. These are the most effective ways to repel and fight off any disturbing energies.

PROTECTION EXERCISE 1:
GROUNDING AND BALANCING YOUR ENERGY

It is important to be centered and well grounded before beginning any sort of protection meditation or visualization. It is very common to have more energy in one part of your body and not enough in another part. Doing this exercise will help you to create a balanced and steady flow of energy so that you can maintain an energetic awareness of your body.

1. Sit in a chair with your spine straight against the back of the chair. This will ensure a proper energy flow up, down, in, and out of the various energy centers, or chakras. Close your eyes and place your awareness in the middle of your head on your third-eye chakra. Be aware of how your body feels.

2. Breathing is one of the most important elements in any exercise. The breath is your cleansing filter. It is important to realize that when you inhale, you are taking in new energy, and when you exhale, you are letting go of used energy.

3. Place your awareness on the soles of your feet. Imagine that your feet are like tree trunks and that roots extend from the soles of your feet downward into the ground right to the center of the earth.

4. Next, imagine a tube that goes from the base of your spine, through the ground, to the center of the earth. This tube

will be used for the release of any excess energy in your body that you no longer need or want.

5. As you breathe in, imagine green, nurturing Mother Earth energy coming up through the roots of your feet and into your legs, pelvis, stomach, and heart.

6. As you exhale, let go of any excess energy you may feel in your body through the tube that is attached to the base of your spine. See this excess energy as gray or brown, and let it flow down the tube and into the earth.

7. After several breaths in and out, imagine the bright golden light of the sun hovering several feet above your head. This light represents the cosmic energies. As you inhale once more, let the golden rays of the light come through the crown chakra at the top of your head and down your body through your head, neck, shoulders, arms, back, and finally into the heart center. As you envision the earth energies and the cosmic energies coming together, feel them blending in your heart.

PROTECTION EXERCISE 2: RECOGNIZING FOREIGN ENERGY AND GHOSTLY ATTACHMENTS

A woman once complained to me that nothing in her life was going right. "What's wrong with me?" she asked. I took one look at her aura and told her, "It's not *what's* wrong with you, it's *who's* wrong with you. Whose energy are you carrying around with you that is impeding your space and influencing your choices?"

Anyone who thinks of you, or with whom you interact, can leave an indelible impression in your aura. It could be your husband, wife, mother, father, child, employer, employee, or neighbor. Most of these energies are harmless, but some may be a source of physical and emotional aches and pains. This next exercise will help you get rid of these parasitic energies.

1. Start with the grounding and balancing exercise. Remember to keep a steady breathing pattern when doing this exercise.

2. Next, imagine that you are standing behind yourself, looking at your body. As you look at your body, become attuned to the space surrounding it. What does this space look and feel like?

3. With your mind's eye, visualize a blank white screen in front of you. This screen is surrounded by a garden of colorful tulips.

4. Special energy vision goggles are plugged into the screen. Take the goggles and place them over your eyes. These goggles are able to detect energetic intrusions.

5. As you stare at the screen with your goggles, scan your body and the space around it from the top of your head on down. Make sure to take your time. *Do not rush through this step.* Some energy is harder to detect than others.

6. While you scan, notice whether there are certain areas of the body and aura that appear dense, as if some type of matter is attached. When you see these pockets of clumped energy, ask the energy to identify who or what it is. The answer will appear on your screen. If it is the energy of a particular person, you will see his or her face projected on the screen. If it is a ghostly attachment, you should see something projected on your screen. It could be a person's figure or a dark

mass. If the energy is leftover from a particular event or situation, the event will appear on the screen. This step is vital in removing the energy from your space.

7. As you identify the energy on the screen, mentally command this energy to leave your space.

8. Next, imagine the unwanted energy absorbed by the tulips in your garden. As it goes into the tulips and back into Mother Earth, it is transmuted into love.

9. If the energy turns out to be an uninvited ghost, mentally send the ghost a message that it has passed out of the physical world and needs to return to its spiritual home. Tell the ghost to ask for a loving relative to come and take it into the light. If the ghost is cooperative, it will be met by a loved one who will help it cross over to the light. Remember that, without your energy, an earthbound ghost loses power and cannot stay in your space unless you allow it.

PROTECTION EXERCISE 3: GETTING BACK YOUR ENERGY

Have you ever felt totally exhausted at the end of the day even though you didn't do much to feel so tired? Your fatigue may be a sign that you have given away a lot of your energy to people, places, and situations. When you feel depleted, you are out of balance, and your well-being suffers. The following exercise will help you get back the energy you gave away.

1. Sit in a comfortable chair in a place where you will not be disturbed.

2. Begin with the grounding and balancing exercise.

3. Close your eyes. Go back to the beginning of your day, from the time you got out of bed. Remember everything that happened during your day, the people you spoke to, the places you spent time in, and so on.

4. Make sure you focus only on one person and situation at a time. As you see the situation in your mind's eye, be aware of the conversation you shared in person, over the phone, or even through e-mail. Be aware that with each conversation, or even by merely thinking of someone, you left a bit of your energy behind.

5. Next, remember your words and thoughts and see them leaving the person and situation and returning to you.

6. Imagine this energy entering the crown chakra at the top of your head. Envision it as gold stardust coming into your space and filling you with renewed energy.

QUICK AND EASY PROTECTION TECHNIQUES

The Shower of Light

Most people wake up every morning and don't think twice about taking a shower or bath to cleanse the physical body. Well, if you can also get into the routine of cleansing your spiritual body while in the shower, you can start your day clearer and lighter.

As you stand under the shower, close your eyes and imagine the water turning into a waterfall of white light. See the white light flowing through your entire body from your head to your feet. As it flows, it washes away psychic debris and stagnant energy. This unwanted energy flows through your fingertips and toes and right down the drain. At the same time, fresh, clean, powerful energy takes its place. As an added bonus of protection, see this white light surround your entire auric shell, sealing up any cracks and holes so that no harmful energy can intrude into your space.

The Reflective Mirror

This is an exercise to do before entering a place where there may be negative energy and you want to protect yourself from people's thoughts and feelings. Imagine that a 360-degree mirror surrounds your entire body. The reflective side points away from you and therefore shields you. When any thoughts come your way, the mirror will deflect them and they will be returned to their source.

The Cloak

When you want to go somewhere and remain anonymous, imagine that you are wearing a dark-colored cloak that covers your entire body from head to toe. You will be amazed by the results. No one will notice that you are around.

The Bubble

Imagine a large bubble completely surrounding you. Fill the bubble with your favorite colors, ones that represent and reflect your personality and make you feel loved. With each color, mentally say, *This color protects me against any negativity that comes my way.*

Pink Light

Whenever you are concerned about someone, like your child, and want to send him or her instant protection, see the person surrounded by a pink light. The color pink represents unconditional love. By envisioning the person in pink light, you are sending him or her love and protection.

Make 'em Laugh

If you are around negative people and you want to change the energy and make the atmosphere lighter, tell a joke, make a silly face, or change the subject to something they can laugh at. Laughter is one of nature's intrinsic defense mechanisms. It can quickly turn depression or sadness into optimism.

No one is immune to the dark forces in spirit. In fact, a dark energy would love to invade a good person and siphon off all that good energy. Wherever you go, always surround yourself with the white light of spirit, and remember that it takes only a minute or two to protect yourself from human and ghostly psychic vampires.

ELEVEN

An Enlightened Life

Imagine if you told a family living in abject poverty that there was a
treasure of gold under the dirt floor of their shanty. They would only
need to remove the layers of dirt hiding it and they would be rich forever.
In the same way, we are not aware of the treasure of our spiritual nature,
hidden by our own ignorance and delusion.

—First Teaching of Buddha

Over the years I have been interviewed by many reporters from
around the globe, and some of the more forward-thinking ones
have asked a certain question that always gets me: "After all these
years and hundreds of thousands of spiritual messages and findings, do you still find what you do amazing and miraculous?" I
have only one answer: "Yes. Because another mind has been
opened."

So far you have learned something about—and maybe come to
appreciate—the unseen spirits that surround you, as well as
something about the worlds they inhabit. Now that you have
read firsthand accounts of spirit phenomena in this book, perhaps your queries about the afterlife have been answered, and

new ones may have taken their place. Perhaps your mind has been opened to a brand-new perspective on life, death, and what lies in between. I certainly hope so.

When I first began communicating with dead people, I was like a child in a candy store. It was a true adventure each time I worked because, being very new to the scene, I never knew whether spirits would show up, or if they did, whether I would be able to see them and understand what they had to say to me. I often wondered how people would find out about me and whether I could earn a living from this work. Twenty years ago, mediums were not as popular as they are today. Actually, in those days it was rare to find a decent medium. All I knew was that I needed to be true to myself and follow the guidance I received from the other side. If I was indeed where I belonged, then there would be nothing to worry about. After all, my work was a plan derived from the spirit world, and I was merely the voice box. Being naturally inquisitive, I found that hearing tales from dead people was a perfect arrangement. So I threw caution to the wind and threw myself into my work. I've enjoyed every minute of it ever since. It is not too far-fetched to say that I have probably experienced, heard, seen, felt, and witnessed every death scenario imaginable and been involved in every possible type of family dynamic.

Initially, I loved my work as much as I did because it was so profound. To sit with a person and direct messages from their deceased loved ones, to watch a depressed, lonely, grief-stricken individual become entirely transformed and made whole right before my eyes, was deeply moving. When I asked clients to describe their experiences, they often couldn't find the appropriate words. One woman, however, once looked straight into my eyes and said, "It was like seeing the light of God."

These connections gave people a new lease on life and a better understanding of themselves and the world in general. Of course, I already had a strong belief system before starting this work. All my life, I have known that we survive death. So when ghosts conveyed evidential details to prove their existence to loved ones, not only were the messages very much needed for my clients, but they also enabled me to learn to attune myself to the spiritual dimensions, to decipher the feelings behind the messages, and to sense the nuances in between the words. My work opened my mind and taught me a whole new attitude toward living.

When you have been touched by the eternal truths of the spiritual dimensions, you cannot possibly go back to the old way of living. Everything I thought about life completely changed. It was if I had been driving a car all my life and then suddenly discovered that I could take a plane to get to my destination. Once I experienced flying, I couldn't deny that it existed. I was able to see the world from thirty thousand feet, and with this new perspective, my knowledge of the world expanded.

Life is about change and growth. Change is the only constant we have. This being said, having spiritual knowledge is not enough. We must also possess a certain amount of faith, trust, and courage to step out of limited belief systems and self-imposed expectations and try a brand-new experience.

Knowledge is power, and awareness is truth. I have learned that when one seeks truth, one has to become responsible for oneself.

You, the reader, have come to a fork in the road, and there is a choice you must make. You can think of this book as an informative and entertaining guide to the world of ghosts and return to your everyday existence with the same mind-set you had before you picked it up. Or you can continue your journey of discovery and open your mind and heart to the very evident reality that ghosts are as real as you are and someday you will be one too. Yes, the phenomenon is amazing, but even more amazing are the astounding insights and simple truths the ghost world has bestowed on me so that I might share these principles with you and

bring you back to your spiritual source. For now, you are temporarily living in a physical shell in a temporary physical environment. If you do utilize the ideas in this book, your life will
change dramatically.

Which road will you choose?

I sincerely hope you have the courage to choose the road less
traveled and explore these insights. In some small way, they may
resonate in your soul.

THE HIGHER SELF

As a being, you are made of many parts. It is ludicrous to believe
that your soul is limited in any way. A soul is *not* human. It comprises vibrations and frequencies that go way beyond the physical
realm. Each vibration and frequency has a distinct appearance.
Your body is at the lowest end of the soul's frequencies. It is
dense and slow-moving. At the highest end of the soul's frequency is the purest part of you. It is your "Higher Self."

The Higher Self is your *true* divine nature. It has been referred
to as the "God-Self" or the "Christ consciousness." It connects
you directly to the spiritual realms and transcends your limited
consciousness. The Higher Self is one of joy, love, compassion,
and happiness. The Higher Self contains the unpolluted and
wholesome elements of your soul that are just waiting to be discovered and expressed. Whenever you say the words "I love you"
to another, you are bringing forth the elements of your Higher
Self.

The Higher Self is different from the "lower self," or "ego self,"
because the latter is part and parcel of the "human" being. The
ego self is completely focused on itself; if misused or unbalanced,
this self becomes trapped in the illusions of the physical world
and desires things it cannot have. There are many stories of
people who set out to amass great financial fortunes because they

think it will bring them true happiness. Then what happens? In spite of their wealth, they are still unhappy. They have fulfilled their desire only to discover that it is empty and unfulfilling. If these same people were to give most of their wealth away to benefit those less fortunate, their souls would feel fulfilled in their desire for happiness because unconditional giving comes from the Higher Self.

How difficult is it to move beyond the lowly desires of the ego self and become aware of the higher elements of our true being? Remember that first and foremost you are already spirit. Your Higher Self already exists. You are remembering what you already know. On one level, you are reminding or reprogramming yourself to come into this awareness. The path to a higher state of consciousness is easily achieved with ongoing meditative practice. By engaging in a program on a regular basis, you can transcend the lower aspects of yourself and raise your vibration.

Along with meditation, I also find it beneficial to surround myself with things I love. For instance, I love flowers and gardens, so I choose to go outside and take part in that which brings me joy and love. The Universal Law of "like attracts like" is key in understanding that our environment influences us in profound and enlightening ways. Merely by watering my garden and planting flowers, I am brought into a state of beauty and oneness with all that surrounds me.

MINDFULNESS

As thinking beings, our minds are constantly running some kind of commentary about the reality of the world around us as well as the world within us. To be mindful is to keep the mind from wandering so as to gain a focus on or awareness of the present moment. In my workshops, I often describe the simple truth of mindfulness in this way: The past has already happened, there is nothing you can do about it, so why give it "worry energy"? The future has yet to happen, so there is nothing about it to be concerned about. The only thing you can control is the present moment. As the spiritual teacher and author Eckhart Tolle says, mindfulness is "living in the now." By bringing your focus back to the "now" moment, you can begin to experience the fullness of your inner and outer realities and make a conscious decision about how you want to use your thoughts. Do your thoughts have merit? Are they building something positive for your life experience? Are your thoughts trivial, judgmental, or invalid?

When I started the practice of mindfulness—and believe me, I had to practice daily until it became a habit—it really was amazing to witness how much garbage came out of my head. As I analyzed my thoughts, I noticed that many of them were based on insecurity, fear, and judgment. On the flip side, I had many creative, imaginative, forgiving, compassionate, and loving thoughts as well. I also noticed that I was in a habit of picking up other people's energy and making their issues mine. Interestingly, when I was with a group of people or in a particular situation, I would often prejudge the people or the situation before experiencing it. This was especially difficult for me because, as an intuitive individual, I am constantly receiving impressions, so I had to use enormous discernment to distinguish between my ego mind and something coming to me from spirit. I had to learn to be in the moment and not judge it. When I did manage to be in the present moment, however, I noticed how much more fun I had and how much more freedom I felt.

Often people think that they can only be truly happy by changing the circumstances in their outer world, but I have found that once you begin to release judgments, attachments, and old habits, they are replaced by happiness. When you don't hold on to these things, you have more room for happiness.

Judgment is a difficult thing to let go of because, when we judge something or someone, we are giving it life. When we step outside of judgment and let someone just be, we start to observe life without getting caught up in the drama.

I am often asked if one must meditate to understand mindfulness. The answer is no. I know that a lot of people have a difficult time meditating and don't want to be so formal about it. You can be mindful every day in the ordinary situations that come up. For instance, I practice mindfulness by sitting in the garden and looking at a tree. The weather may change, but the tree just stands there. I know the tree is not analyzing the weather conditions, but merely experiencing them. I also experience mindfulness by observing the goldfish swimming around the small pond in my garden. The goldfish are not judging their environment; they are merely swimming around in the water and being goldfish.

I recommend that you get into the rhythm of practicing simple mindfulness every day. Taking charge of your thoughts will bring you unprecedented freedom.

THE HUMAN EXPERIENCE

As spiritual beings, we chose to come back to this earth at this exact time to encounter all of the opportunities that will propel us and the human race forward in earth's evolution. When we decided to revisit earth and be human again, we also decided to take on all the responsibilities of life. The human condition is a myriad of paradoxes and contradictions. Our natural state as spirits is one of expanded consciousness. We have a constant knowingness and the power to create with thought and ideas. The *secret* that has escaped us for centuries is remembering our divine nature. All the power we will ever need is right inside us. Without the realization that we are spiritual beings having a human experience, we remain in denial of the truth. We become victims of circumstances rather than creators of our fates.

When we enter this dimension that is limited in scope, our identities are somehow elusive. Most of us attempt the sojourn looking outside of ourselves to find answers. We tend to look to others to validate and measure our own worthiness and our truth. However, who knows us better than ourselves? All of the answers we want to know are found nowhere else but inside our own hearts.

When we take on human flesh, we close the curtain on the memories of prior life experiences in order to start over with a clear conscience. This is really a moment of grace that is given to us by God. For if we were aware of our past journeys on this earth, we would spend our valuable time obsessing over the rights and wrongs of other lives rather than living this lifetime and evolving as spiritual beings. By starting over each lifetime, we are free to choose the reality we want to experience.

When we reincarnate on earth, we bring with us a blueprint of all that has gone before. By choosing various people and situations with which to experience life, we are forced into situations that expedite our soul's growth. Only the material world can offer us so many opportunities to learn our lessons and provide immediate feedback on our actions, mistakes, and achievements.

We are human, rational beings encapsulated in a spiritual, unlimited consciousness. In fact, we are our consciousness. Everything we create is through consciousness. I have incredible respect and admiration for the hip-hop artist Mary J. Blige. She is a remarkable example of finding the power within to change reality. She came from the "hood," a place filled with drugs and crime. One day she assessed her life and her neighborhood and told herself, "I am getting out of here and making something of myself." She says that she prayed to God—or as I like to say, found her inner spiritual power and took responsibility for changing her reality. And she did just that. She is one of the most successful female musicians in history. When Mary J. Blige made a choice to get out of her negative surroundings, she did so with a desire not only to achieve success and good things for herself and her family but also to teach others, through her success, that it was possible.

I have found over and over again in my work that the number-one regret for most ghosts is that they didn't believe in themselves when on earth. They wish someone had told them that they were immense souls living human experiences. If they had only known this power while they were alive, they might have believed in themselves more and might have lived different lives.

As a spirit having a human experience, you can choose to not merely exist but to be fully conscious and aware of living in a limited world. When you take a conscious part in life and its multitudes of choices, you won't let life happen *to* you—you will make life happen *for* you.

THE POWER OF THOUGHT

Everything begins with a thought. A thought is alive and as solid as a rock or a piece of furniture. Thoughts are communicated by waves or vibrations. The physical materialization of thought takes form in words. If people could witness how effective and real their thoughts are, they would be in utter shock. When we pass into the spirit world, part of our life review is to witness *all* the thoughts we had during our lives on earth. We are held accountable for these thoughts.

General Thoughts

Imagine that you are sitting by a pond and you throw a pebble into the water. What happens? Instantly, ripples flow outward in all directions. Thoughts are like ripples: they resonate in the minds of others. When someone transmits positive and loving thoughts, these thoughts are received by others and produce similar thoughts of love. Alternatively, someone whose heart is filled with hatred and jealousy transmits discordant thoughts and stirs up hatred and jealousy in the minds and hearts of those with similar thoughts.

Sending Thoughts

A thought is a living thing. When you think it, it's as if you're shooting a bullet into someone's energy field. I have seen thousands of people come to my workshops with auras filled with psychic debris and thought forms from their family members, friends, co-workers, and neighbors. There is strength and power in thoughts, and we must learn to use them wisely and for everyone's benefit. "With your thoughts you can either build or destroy."

Positive Thoughts

A wonderful example of using your thoughts in a positive and loving way is when you send prayers of healing to another. Prayers and thoughts of healing are the whispers of unconditional love directed at someone to bring about a positive reaction in them. In all my group meditations, I direct positive energy toward everyone in the room. It's amazing how differently people feel after the meditation is over. They feel more open and loving.

Negative Thoughts

The same is true for using the creative force of thought in a negative way. Curses are an example of sending negative thoughts. A curse goes out to a person or place with all the emotional negativity behind it and attaches to that person or place. It can also fuel the negativity that already exists in that person and place. It is important to note that if you send out negative thoughts, you will receive back what you have created.

The Intention of Thoughts

The dictionary defines *intention* as: "conception of a thing formed *first* by the direct application of the mind to the individual object, idea, or image. It is a stretching or bending of the mind toward an object." Another word we could substitute for *intention* is *manifestation*. The objective is the same. An intention gives the thought its direction. You state what you choose to create with your thought. To get the most benefit out of your intention, you must make it extremely specific and clear. You do not want to leave any room for generalities. You want to manifest your thought into the material world exactly as you designed it, so never leave out the details. You might be quite surprised by what you get if you do. Remember that, with intention, you are shaping your thought. Imagine that you are building a house. You have the thought of the house, the design, the size, and the location. All these intentions are bringing your thought one step closer to manifestation. In this case, it would be the foundation of the house. How can you build a house without a foundation? So intention forms the thought.

Thought Focus

Remember that you are a creative individual and that whatever you focus your mind on will come to pass. It is amazing how this works. If you want something in your life, first you must think of it, put your intention behind it, and keep your focus on it. It is almost like baking a cake. The thought is in the oven, but you have to keep it baking with *belief*. You have to see your thought manifesting and becoming real. The ingredients, or specifics, of your thought help to clarify and expedite its manifestation.

Emotions Are Needed

The more emotion you put into your thought, the more power it has to manifest. Emotion is the extra energy needed to propel your thought into reality. When you visualize your thought becoming a reality, how does it make you feel emotionally? This works all the time. Children play "make-believe," but they are living their game as if it were real. You too must play make-believe so that your dream becomes real. You have the right to live a happy and purposeful life, and it begins with making the correct spiritual choices. After all, whatever you do in this life you bring with you into the next.

THE POWER OF FEAR

Fear is probably the most powerful negative emotion we have. It has the strength to entangle minds, to motivate, to terrify, and even to stop life. I always use the following example in my workshops. Life is a series of choices. Each choice reflects a belief based on either love or fear. These choices define who we are, how we want to live our lives, and how we want to be perceived. If we choose to love, then we are using the natural energy of life. If we choose to fear, then we are operating in an unnatural state. Love is an energy that pulls all things together. Fear separates.

Look at a specific time in your life when you had to make a big life choice—like getting married, getting divorced, moving, changing a job or a career path, or starting a family. Did you make your choice because it was expected or because you truly loved what you were doing? In other words, have your choices been made from fear or love? Many of us make certain choices because we feel others want us to make that choice, not because it is what we truly want. Because most of us want to feel accepted by our loved ones and to fit in with our peers and society, we sometimes go with the unnatural choice rather than what our spirit wants.

If you discover that you have made decisions based on fear, then you also know that you are not living the happiest life you could. If you choose from love, you are happy. Fear usually causes everything to be out of sync: things don't seem to fit together, and you don't feel like you fit in. You may even feel that you are missing out on a major part of life. The energy of fear seems to hold you back. When I clairvoyantly scan someone's body and discover they have fear energy, what I'm sensing is that the life force in their body has slowed down; sometimes it has come to a complete halt. The opposite is also true. Love causes the energy to flow freely and evenly throughout the body.

When people make major life choices based on fear, I have found that fear creeps into every aspect of their lives. They have what I call a "fear-based" life, meaning that all of their thoughts are fearful and inadequate and their entire outlook on life and themselves is that way.

Every thought is based on either love or fear. When you have fear-based energy, you attract others on that same level. Therefore, nothing will be honest in your life, and the people you draw to yourself won't be self-realized. Sometimes a fear-based solution might seem easier, but it will be accompanied by unforeseen pain and heartache.

We are usually guided and taught how to make choices by our parents. Many times we continue making decisions based on what we were taught. However, our inner selves may lead us in a different direction from the one dictated by our parents' desires and beliefs.

Is all fear bad for us? Certainly not. There is healthy fear and unhealthy fear. For instance, if I am on the highway driving and notice that the driver in front of me is weaving from side to side, I stay back for fear that he may lose control of his car and hit me. This is a healthy fear because I am protecting my life. Unhealthy fear is fear of something that cannot hurt you. For instance, if you worry about the stock market going down, this is an unhealthy fear because you cannot control the stock market. The only thing you can do is to take your money out of it. Things that you are obsessed about but cannot change tend to be unhealthy or irrational fears.

Then, of course, there are other types of fears, such as fear of success, fear of death, fear of acceptance, fear of a terrorist attack, fear of being alone. These fears are part of life, but we need to put them in proper perspective. We can use these types of fear to motivate ourselves or to change our lives, to grow and to learn rather than stifle ourselves.

Organizations of all sorts control people through the use of fear. Most of what we hear and see on TV or the Internet instills fear in us. It is imperative that we have a strong sense of self and that we think about our choices before making them.

It is important to remember that earthbound ghosts, as well as the basest of humans, live off of our fear energy. The more fear you manifest, the more life you give them.

People ask me if I believe in demons, the devil, and so on. I say, not necessarily. However, I do believe the mind can create anything it wants. I have noticed that after I cleanse a house of negative energy the occupants will often remark, "I feel great," or, "I feel as though I have my power back." And they do.

THE POWER OF LOVE

The energy of love is the most powerful, natural force in the Universe. Love binds everything together and permeates everything in the Universe. It is difficult to define *love* because it envelops so much of life itself. Love heals, enlightens, and builds. It is the one element that I can say transcends death. Many times I am asked by people, "Do spirits know I am thinking of them?" The answer is always, "Yes!" More importantly, spirits feel the love that we have for them. It is this force of love that binds souls together through lifetimes. The reason I do my work is to demonstrate that love never dies.

When communicating with ghosts or clearing haunted places, focus on love. It can immediately change a wayward spirit or stagnant energy. Its vibration quickens everything and brings it to a higher level of consciousness. It is interesting that whenever I bring through a loving message from a ghost, because of the limitations of the physical world, I can only bring through a tenth of what the total feeling is.

Love is difficult for many people to recognize and accept. It seems like a stranger to them. Could that difficulty stem from their upbringing? Yes, possibly, but many other factors could be involved as well.

When I work with clients who have no sense of loving themselves, I do a couple of exercises that seem to give them a completely new understanding of themselves and a new sense of who they are. I start by asking them to tell me one thing they love to do. Let's say my client is a woman who loves to buy herself a new dress now and then. I ask her to visualize going out and buying a dress, trying it on, and looking in the mirror. I ask her, "How does the dress make you feel?" Once she connects with that feeling, I have her analyze it, make it real, and even give the feeling a name. Then I ask her to make a list of personal attributes that give her that same feeling and urge her to look at that list every day and add to it. Within a week's time of looking each day at the attributes that give her this wonderful feeling, she will have achieved a new self-awareness.

Another very successful exercise I have used with clients is to have them write on a piece of paper, "I love you [insert their own name]," and tape it to the bathroom mirror. They must repeat this statement out loud three times in the morning and three times in the evening. There is a unique healing effect that takes place when we focus love on ourselves. This exercise also gives those who try it a keen sense of self-esteem and self-appreciation.

When we love unconditionally, we use energy in its highest possible form. When we love without rules and restrictions and accept someone or something the way it is, love is able to grow and evolve.

I often think about the world's religions and ethnicities. It seems to me that God, or the Universe, has wondrously created each of us as a facet of a diamond: each facet is different, and together the facets form a diamond that is brilliant and beautiful. It is the uniqueness that makes the diamond beautiful. Every belief system is beautiful in its knowledge. No one is better than anyone else. This is merely the illusion of the physical world. Only when we can celebrate our diversity and love one another unconditionally will there be true peace on this planet. Because we have not learned love yet, we still kill our own species. This puts Planet Earth very low on the spiritual evolutionary scale.

Each one of us can only do the best we can in our own lives to demonstrate love whenever possible. If enough of us send out love, the energy will permeate the ignorance and darkness of those beings lost in their limited mind-sets. Even in that darkness, however, the energy of love will find them. Perhaps the living can learn from the dead and realize that the divine ingredient of love can free us all from the darkness. Then we can enter a new beginning of understanding in a physical world illuminated by a heavenly light.

Acknowledgments

BBB—Never knew the meaning of life till you showed me how to love.

Linda Tomchin—Thank you, as always, for giving the ghosts a voice.

Sam—Who understands things in her own way and that's a good thing . . . right?

The "Kids"—You make me proud to call you my children. Live, love, and prosper!

Cammy Farone—I can never express my appreciation for all you do. Your undying devotion to the Web site and assistance to others to step out of their pain is honorable.

Kelley Kreinbrink—I appreciate your being there to pick up the pieces and put them back together.

Bernadette—You are indeed an angel and healer. From the four-legged creatures to the two-legged ones, thank you for sharing your kindness and compassion.

Ruth—You are truly the meaning of family. Thank you for being in mine.

Christian—You are just too much! Thank you for the friendship, the laughs, and the love. I will leave you with that!

Joerdie Fisher—Mom, thank you for living your truth and giving others the courage to look inside to find theirs.

Marilyn Jensen—Blessings to my one and only Ruby Star.

Peter Redgrove—Thank you for sharing each step on this earthly sojourn. One day we will look back from the other side and know it was worth it.

Mary Ann Saxon—I am blessed to call you a true and honest friend. Christmas will always be ours.

Cindy Schacher—With all your love, support, and sparkles, you would give Tinkerbell a run for her money.

Mary Ann Winkowski—You are and always will be my favorite ghost-buster. Thanks for keeping your feet on the ground while others are lost in space.

Scott Schwimer—Thank you for always being there through the years. I am blessed to know you.

Gideon Weil—Heaven must have sent you. You are the best editor an author could ever have. Thank you for all your encouragement.

To all the ghosts I met on earth—see you when I get to heaven.

About the Author

James Van Praagh is considered a pioneer of the mediumship movement throughout the world, and has been recognized as one of the most accurate spiritual mediums working today. He is a celebrated lecturer, author, producer and unique intuitive.

The number one *New York Times* best-selling author of *Talking to Heaven, Reaching to Heaven, Healing Grief, Heaven and Earth, Looking Beyond* and *Meditations,* his books have found international acclaim, and have been translated into over twenty-five languages in thirty countries. Van Praagh is also a frequent guest on *Larry King Live* and has shared his expertise on numerous television and radio shows and specials, including *Oprah, Unsolved Mysteries, The Other Side, Paranormal Borderline, 20/20, 48 Hours, Maury, The O'Reilly Factor, Possessed Possessions, John Edward Cross Country, Coast to Coast, Chelsea Lately,* A & E's *We See Dead People* and many more. He was a part-time correspondent on *Entertainment Tonight* and *The Insider* and also hosted his own internationally syndicated show *Beyond with James Van Praagh.* Van Praagh is also a successful producer for CBS, creating the mini-series *Living with the Dead* based on his life, and *The Dead Will Tell* staring Anne Heche and Eva Longoria.

Currently, he is the co-executive producer of CBS's number one drama *The Ghost Whisperer* starring Jennifer Love Hewitt. His incredible spirit messages and award-winning meditations have brought solace, peace, and spiritual insights, changing millions' view of both life and death. He is also in high demand as a speaker, giving sold-out lectures, seminars, and training workshops across the world. Visit the author on line at www.vanpraagh.com.